STOLEN
HERITAGE

Blood and Stones

NANA ABA

NEWMAN SPRINGS PUBLISHING
320 Broad Street
Red Bank, NJ 07701

First originally published by Newman Springs Publishing 2021

ISBN 978-1-64531-462-2 (Paperback)
ISBN 978-1-64531-463-9 (Digital)

Printed in the United States of America

To my sister Sylvia, your strength gives me hope.
I pray you continue to evolve and embody the
spirit of excellence. Never give up!

To my African brothers and sisters back
home, you are not forgotten.

To those who were lucky enough to receive a second chance,
make the most of the opportunity you've been given.

Immigrants across the nations, regardless of your plight you can
overcome the atrocities you experience. Do not let your history
overshadow your future.

And finally to all of my women worldwide, your worth is not and
can never be measured by your gender or the color of your skin.
Success is blind to such matters.

Love, Nana Aba

Contents

Acknowledgments

If God is for you, who can be against you? None of this would have been possible without His grace. His countless favor forever humbles me. Thank you, Lord.

To my mother: when you read this, I want you to see vividly the woman you raised, and I want you to be proud and know I couldn't have accomplished this if I wasn't the person you raised me to be.

To my siblings: Sylvia and Emmanul and Sylvia, I love you both Jay Sims, Thank you for always answering when I call.

Valery, Kiara, Telecia, to say thank you is an understatement. You are a true definition of great friendship and a great support system. Thank you.

To Mr. and Mrs. Keefer, The opportunity you gave me when I needed it the most made an impact in my life and I will forever be grateful for your love and compassion.

To the khakis who made it count; Commander Kamara, I love you so much and I'm eternally appreciative for the passion and attitude of perseverance you continue to instill in me.

Master Chief Cason, the lessons you taught me has positively impacted my life. I thank you.

Finally, to everyone I encountered during the writing of this book, Our expeirience aligned me perfectly as part of God's plan for this momment to arrive. Thank you for being part of my story. May God continue to use you for his work.

Letter to Black Women

Your hair is not unprofessional. It's not too curly or kinky. God made you this way purposely to stand out so, do not seek to blend in. Your attitude isn't too abrasive or "bitchy" You project power and some people can't cope with that, but that's not your problem. You're not aggressive, you have passion! Something it takes others a lifetime to find. Your complexion isn't the problem, The problem lies with close-minded people, so be patient with yourself. The universe will open up to you.

In the meantime, break down barriers, wear your wild Afro with pride, overcome boundaries, be as beautifully dark as you are and embrace your true self. Don't let society's stipulations and expectations of who you *"should"* be get in your way of self-love and success.   With much love,
                         Another Black Woman

The Genesis

One fine day, as the morning sun shone brightly over the Pentagon, I received an honor befitting the pleasant weather. My team and I had just returned from our five-month-long deployment and my CO, Commander Breeden, had selected me to be awarded the Silver Star. After the traumatic childhood I had endured, this ceremony was a ground-breaking and cathartic moment in my life. Surrounded by my friends and colleagues from all military branches, I finally felt the sense of accomplishment I longed for. I always felt like I was meant for something greater than what I had planned for myself and on that day every single word of the speech I delivered remaians alive in my memory.

"Here is to beating the odds. To get here, a man must simply do his part. A woman must do twice as much, but a Black woman must work three times harder, plus overtime, to achieve just as much. Women are more than they can imagine and therefore, must not be defined by our limits becuase we don't have any. If society had its way, someone else would be receiving this award, I say to hell with society. We remain limitless and unsilenced.

When you let your environment define you, you allow insur-mountable hindrance to your growth. As a woman, I cannot allow that, but morst importantly as a Black woman, I do not have that luxury. I must not conform. I must rise and continue to fight for those who cannot fight for themselves.

It is a great honor to be promoted to lieutenant's rank and to become the first Black woman to receive this honorable award. Thank you."

*****

I ended my speech to loud applause and joined my friends at the table. That morning, I tied my curly dark-brown hair back in a bun. As I gazed around the room, I took notice of the shortage of people who looked like me. I felt sick at the lack of not only women but specifically women of color who were present. And yet a sense of joy filled my heart. I, Asha Yaa Asantewaa Osei, the only daughter of the reigning King of the Ashanti people in Ghana, had earned a place among the best.

As the crowd fell into silence once again, I became lost in my thoughts. I drifted back to my childhood and my birthplace. The way sun's glow would overtake the sky, the strong winds would blow the leaves of the many trees outside my window. Leaving home brought me more pain than I thought I could endure. We all carry memories from our youth that are embedded within us forever; for me, my departure from Ghana is still evident in my mind. The local tribes had been waging war with one another over ethnic disputes. There was so much suffering and destruction inflicted by men upon men, all in the name of traditions. What I witnessed created an emotional scar in my heart that is far deeper than other pain I could bear. Till this day, I still can't undrstand my father's decision to save my life.

I was shaken out of my reminiscing by a phone call from my mother. I smiled as I picked up. There was apparent panic in her shivering voice. "Home! You need to come home!" she cried without pleasantries.

My mind sprang alert, and my heart started racing. The queen of the Ashanti was known to her people as Obaahene Efia Asantewaa, but to me, she was just Mum. She addressed me in one of the most dominant languages in Ghana—the Asante Twi. We belonged to the land where life first began, so when we spoke, it felt as though we were breathing life into our words.

I could hear she was utterly breathless. "What happened Mum? What's going on?" I asked her in an alarming tone. I stepped outside away from the crowd so I could speak more freely. As I listened anxiously, my mum quickly clarified that my presence was urgently needed. After we hung up, I immediately left the event and began planning for the journey home. The dark memories of my war-torn childhood weighted my mind.

The circumstances of my flight from Ghana had forced me to keep my royal identity hidden all this time, even from my closest friends. I had spent years working and living with these people, yet they didn't have the faintest idea of who I am.

*****

My friends, Maya and Adelaide joined me in the reception area of Pentagon hotel as waited for our fourth. At twenty-eight, Maya was the eldest of us. She was a Hispanic American who held the rank of Lieutenant Commander, one of the highest-ranking women within our office. Although our histories and reasons for seeking refuge in America were nothing alike, as Immigrants, we shared some common issues in the workplace. In contrast to Maya, Adelaide flaunted her rank proudly. As a lieutenant junior grade at the tender age of twenty-five, she has alot of passion.

While we waited, the conversation between the two of them rotated between fashion, television shows, and geopolitics. As it often did. As they discussed the upcoming Arab Fashion Week, Maya remarked on all the conflicts in that part of the world. I was immediately triggered and my mind traveled back to my past once more.

Images of my younger self twirled in front of my eyes; I watched an adolescent girl reaching out to the glistening ocean waters, extending her hand toward the setting sun, longing to go back home and felt my heart break. Regardless of how difficult my life in the United States was, I owed my family the effort to break the barriers and boundaries my culture tried to impose on me. Though these traumas happened a long time ago, the memories of it all were e bound to me forever. The blood-streaked streets and smoke-filled horizons of my birthplace were experiences that formed me. After being graced with the opportunity of a new secure life, failure was not an option for me.

My friends attempted to bring me back into the conversation, but I remained distracted. Shrugging off my unresponsiveness, Maya and Adelaide continued talking until Jelani joined us. He and I had been dating for some years. Jay had joined the navy through the ROTC program and was commissioned around the same time I was. Although we both held the Lieutenant's rank, I was an intel officer while he worked in our commanding officer's office. He could never really explain what he doe A year older than me at age twenty-six, he was very mature and the most supportive man that any woman could ask for. His arrival shook me from the deep abyss of my memories, or were they nightmares?

Since my group was now complete, I plunged in and revealed my plans. "I'm going back home tomorrow. To Ghana, I mean."

Their eyebrows rose, and their expressions took on surprise and concern. Adelaide was the first to respond. "Why so, suddenly?"

"I miss home. Plus my mum needs me," I replied, hoping that they would not see through my lie.

"Well, we're coming with you," Asha was her prompt toreply.

"Absolutely," Jay added. "There's no way I'm going to stay behind while you make such a long trip. I'm coming with you."

Even though I wasn't quite ready to take him home, I could tell his mind was already made up, and I didn't have the time or energy to fight him so I agreed reluctantly.

"But what are we going to do about work? You guys know we can't leave," Maya objected. "We have to plan how to go about this carefully. I don't mind coming with you, but let's sit down and think things through first."

It made sense for Maya to be concerned about the preparations. Being the most senior of us, she would have the most to lose if any-thing were to happen regarding this trip.

After further discussion, Maya's concerns were appeased, and we formed a concrete plan for the trip. "Now that we have all that figured out, I think we should meet at a hotel close to the airport in the morning before our flight," I suggested.

"Why don't we just meet at the airport?" Adelaide asked.

"Because I need to discuss something with you guys first."

"Okay then"

Next, I assigned their tasks. "Adelaide, you're in charge of the plane tickets. Maya, make sure Commander has everything he needs from us topproved.

"Well, what about me?" Jay inquired.

"Women are much better at getting things done. That's why she didn't ask you to do anything," Adelaide joked and all laughed.

*****

A few hours later, I called my friends to inquire about their packing progress. I assumed they were ready because I definately Ishould have by now, but I but too nervous. I had no idea what to even pack. Everything I held close to my heart awaited me in Ghana, including the very clothes I'd be wearing. Although we'd initially planned on meeting up an hour before we had to be at the airport, I changed my mind, the secret was holding burdened me. The sooner I got it over with, the better. So I picked up my phone and called Jay.

"Hello?" his soothing voice echoed from the other side.

"Hey you! I need to ask you for a favor."

"Okay, what's up?"

"Instead of waiting till the morning, can we meet at the Marriott tonight? In about an hour?" Silence spread on the other end of the line. "Um…hello?"

"Sure. I'm almost done here, anyway."

"Can you pick up Maya and Adelaide as well? Bring them to the hotel with you," I requested.

He agreed, and I quickly pulled myself together for the conversation we were about to have. The clock was striking at 7:00 p.m. when we all seated ourselves comfortably on a couple of sofas near reception.

"How long is the trip from Washington to Kumasi?" Adelaide asked.

Maya answered before I could open my mouth. "Well, it's supposed to take no longer than twelve hours. Since the flight departs tomorrow at 6:00 a.m., we should reach Kumasi somewhere around 8:00 p.m., Kumasi nighttime."

She was precise about everything.

"Our flight isn't directly to Kumasi, so it might take longer," Jay chimed in.

"Yes, we'll land in Accra first and then switch over to a short flight to Kumasi." I looked at Jay, and he smiled back at me.

I was already getting restless with the small talk. Just thinking about the flight made me nervous. The girls began discussing how the domestic Ghanaian airlines were known for their excessive delays. Jay was sitting beside me while Maya and Adelaide were across from us.

Realizing that this was as good an opportunity as any, I reached into my handbag and took out a piece of paper. The excitement on their faces was seized by confusion, and they fell silent as I placed the paper upside down on my lap. They watched me play around with my fingers and struggled to say something. Of the three, Adelaide was the most impatient one. She was much more observant than she let on; undoubtedly, she noticed the change in my body language and brimmed with questions. Maya and Jay remained calm.

My throat went dry. I laid one hand on the paper and decided that it was now or never. I had spent so many years keeping my identity hidden; I felt odd recognizing it now.

I finally mustered up the courage to speak. "Look, I'm going to tell you something very very serious It's probably going to sound strange," I began and then took a long pause. "I've been lying to you."

"Really? Let me guess: you're not American. You're a spy for some other country." Adelaide remarked sarcastically and Maya chuckled nervously.

Jay leaned away from me teasingly. From the earliest days of our relationship, I had been honest with him about who I was and made him swear to protect my secret. It was clear from his body language that he knew where this conversation was going. His curiosity about Maya and Adelaide's imminent reactions to the news glinted brightly in his eyes.

"Well, I've been hiding who I am. I'm from a royal bloodline, a member of the Ashanti royal family."

An awkward silence followed my unexpected confession. Maya's face was full of shock, while Adelaide stared at me blankly.

"I'm the only daughter of Nana Adofo Yaw Osei III, the current king of the Ashanti people in Ghana. I have an elder brother."

Maya's jaw dropped. "Maya! Are you all right?" Jay placed his hands on her shoulders to coax her back to reality.

"I'm all right, just confused." Maya shook herself. "So…what is it like being a princess?"

"Well, for starters, you need to sign this nondisclosure agreement so not only my identity remains a secret between us but so does everything you see and hear while you're in the palace. Understood? If you breach this, even I can't help you." I gestured at the paper. As close as we were, it bothered me I had to make them do this, but I had no choice.

I could tell they were hurt. I just wished they understood how awful I felt about this. I knew it appeared as though I didn't trust them, but the nondisclosure agreement was non-negotiable. My family, specifically my father, would have my heads if I didn't get them on board.

After they signed, I told them the real reason I was returning home. My father was seriously sick, and my family needed me. I explained to them how I had ended up in the States in the first place. Then I revealed that my reason for joining the navy had been to gain military intel on an operation in Ghana, which had resulted in many of our ancient native artifacts stolen. Most of them were now in museums, when their rightful place was in the palace. My father wanted these artifacts back. Jay, though already aware of my identity, had no idea about my real intentions. He and the girls were taken aback and probably felt betrayed by all this information.

Adelaide found her voice first. "Are you crazy? You realize you're an officer, right? Not to mention a US citizen. You signed a contract! You want to get us all court-martialed?"

"We're all going to jail," Maya added with her hands to her forehead.

Jay just stared, his face contorted into a painful expression. He was upset.

I sighed, "Look, this country saved me. I will never deny that, and I will forever be grateful; But my country is still my country. I will always be indebted to it. I cannot forget the crimes initiated against it. Those past sins are yet to be forgiven."

I could see my friends were determined to convince me to abort my intentions. While I was proud to serve America, I also was obli-gated by tradition to remain loyal to my roots. "Tell you what, come home with me. You'll soon understand the impact these crimes of slavery and war still have on my country. You'll get why I need those artifacts back. They mean so much more to us than to anyone who might see them sitting in a museum here."

"Well, when you put it like that...now we feel bad," Maya confessed.

"Feel bad?" Adelaide barked. "I stole nothing. I don't feel obligated to understand or pity you just because a long time ago, someone stole from you."

"Someone? You mean your people—White people, right? Because you guys are the ones always stealing shit from other people," I retaliated heatedly. "You guys, first of all—"

Before Adelaide could cut back in, Maya interjected, "Okay! Everyone needs to calm down. We're all friends remember? You're letting history affect you. Adelaide, get your temper in check. This isn't about you. Asha, whatever you do, make damn sure you don't end up dragging us all down. You might have somewhere to go back to, but for us, this is it. We don't have anywhere else. So think of others when you plan to betray the same country that took you in."

Her words cut me. "Of course! I would never do anything to put you or your careers in jeopardy. You have to trust that." I assured them, looking especially at Adelaide.

This assertion convinced them to give the conversation a rest, and with that, we awkwardly went our separate ways.

A quarter past four the next morning, we met at the airport to board our 6:00 a.m. flight. It was a short matter of time before our plane took off. From my window seat, my eyes fixed on the clouds passing by. I could not help but think about how the clouds would look above my homeland. Would everything look the same? It was a long time since I had left.

*****

Two flight later, we landed in Kumasi. As we descended, I gazed out the window again, this time at my beautiful city. The mountains towered on one side, and the beautiful bounty of buildings sprawled on the other. I could no longer suppress my emotions. A familiar wind unsettled my tight curls, and my eyes swelled up with tears. The highland grass around the tarmac danced and swayed. I was happy to have my friends with me, yet sad about the circumstances that prompted me home. My heart was awaiting the royal palace. On the other hand, my friends seemed utterly thrilled to be setting foot in Africa for the first time.

Just a few steps away from the airport's arrival terminal, five people waited for me. Of them, four were royal servants dressed in tribal clothing made of kente fabric. One could always spot our kente material from afar because of its vibrant colors. The royal servants had servitude roles within the palace. None had been forced into servitude, and they could leave our service as they wished. A man stood in front of these maids—Femi, my brother. The last time I saw him, we were barely an adolescent. Now, before me stood a tall and prominent man. Just by looking at his clothing, one could tell he was of royalty.

"Who's that?" Adelaide wondered loudly.

"Don't even!" Maya and I both responded aggressively.

"Well, well, well. Look who decided to come home, finally!" Femi smiled as I approached, widening his arms for a hug. "Welcome home, sister!" He leaned toward me and embraced me warmly.

This hug was long overdue. So, I hugged him back as tightly as I could as I wiped my tears on his shoulder.

On our way to the palace, we drove past the lively Kejetia Market. As usual, the place was bustling with the beloved people of my home-land. At the request of Maya, the cars stopped in front of the market for a while. My friends were eager to explore Kumasi and appreciated the beautiful sights the city offered. Unlike other Ghanaian cities plagued with crumbling heritage, sewage-lined streets, severe pov-erty, and beggars, Kumasi was a model to look toward.

After getting back into our cars, we continued toward our desti-nation. We passed by the Manhyia Palace, built for local rule back in 1925 and once served as the royal palace. My friends snapped a few photos of the grand building. Although this was the first palace that was purposed for the seat of the Asantehene, it was not a residence anymore; it was converted into a museum in the 1990s. I promised my friends that we would explore the market more thoroughly and visit the palace museum later since it was already so late in the day.

King Opuku Ware II built my family's current residence. It was close to Manhyia. As we drove up to my childhood home, I looked at Jay sitting next to me in the back seat. His gaze was fixed upon the sun, which was setting beautifully on the distant horizon. Up where the sky was growing darker, the stars had already come out to play. Our SUVs came to a halt right in front of the palace, and Maya and Adelaide jumped out in excitement. Although I was happy to be back home, my joy was overtaken by my darker thoughts of the situation I was about to confront. Meanwhile, the maids led my friends into the palace to help em settle in.

Though the drive home had been quite enjoyable for my friends and I, I noticed my brother was unusually quiet. Since our reunion at the airport he had spoken only a few words. As my friends were escorted inside the palace, my brother and tood side side. He placed his hands on my shoulder. His silence spoke a thousand words.

The Passage

Holding back the tears in our eyes, my brother and I walked into the palace. Upon entering through the main door, I saw my friends make their way to the back garden and my mother walking toward the main entrance. She rushed over and embraced me in the warmest hug imaginable. I could feel the tears running down her cheeks. She tried her best not to cry, but just like me, she had no luck suppressing her feelings. She took my face in her hands and kissed my forehead. She sighed heavily and said, "*Me ba, akwaaba*," meaning, "Welcome, my daughter."

"Thank you, Mum. Where is he? How is he now?" I inquired with growing concern.

Without speaking further, she grabbed my hand and walked me toward the stairs. We walked upstairs and came to a halt outside a familiar room. It was the room I had grown up sleeping in. As I looked at the door, I remembered the beautifully carved details from my childhood. The door looked just like it had all those years ago. My mum led the way, and we entered my father's chamber. My dad lay idly in bed, with his eyes slightly opened; his eyes already fixed on the door.

"Pa!" I exclaimed as I rushed toward him. I leaned in and hugged him. Tiredly, he gave me half-hug, raising his feeble arms. We spent the entire night talking about my mischieves as a child, and the tribal war in Ghana that led to my departure. I told him alabout the life I had made for myself in the States, my two friends Maya and Adelaide, and the deails of my relationship with Jelani.

Just as I went into details about them, they walked into the room and introduced themselves. They joined us for a while and then left me alone with my dad once again. Our conversation drifted back to the days I had spent at sea operating as an intel officer for missions and whatever else we could think of. Unable to leave his side, I fell asleep right beside him, seated on the floor, with my head rested on his bed. It wasn't long before the morning sun tickled me awake. I was looking forward to starting my day. I would get to show some of Kumasi's most beautiful places to my friends.

We started the day by going back to the Kejetia Market. Maya hadn't had enough of it; it is one of the largest market in West Africa. It's open-air, and haggling masses instilled the place with a sense of total freedom.

"So what do you think of the market?" I asked after we'd roamed around for a while. "I know it was dark outside yesterday, but this is what she looks like in all her glory."

"It's amazing! But I have to admit, I'd probably get lost in here every day," Maya remarked.

"Yes. It's very crowded here," Adelaide said, her voice sounding exhausted.

"If you want somewhere more tranquil, we can go to one of the best parks—the Rattray Park," I said to her and then looked at Jay, who was holding the local Ghanaian souvenirs he'd recently purchased.

When we arrived at the park, I showed them the lake first. Jay loved parks, and he immediately took my hand and dragged me toward him. We sat downat one of the wooden benches to catchup.

Meanwhile, Maya and Adelaide roamed around the park, observing Kumasi's people and their daily activities. Jelani must have noticed my sudden change of mood as I stared across the park. He took my hand and asked if I was okay. "Yeah," I responded reluctantly. They all knew my father's condition worsened with every passing minute. They did their best to support me.

23

Next, we toured the Kumasi Fort, which had been transformed into an armed forces museum in 1953. At the entrance of this red-bricked structure, a line of army tanks served as a spectacle to prospective visitors. Given its hut-like architecture, the museum wasonof a kind. As we entered, I could see the growing curiosity in Maya's eyes. It was not my first visit to this place but it had been a relatively long time since I had visited. I asked the others to stand together so I could take some pictures. "Why aren't you taking any pictures, Asha?" Maya asked.

Adelaide responded, "The girl's from here. She probably owns all of this."

I joined my friends in laughter. We headed home shortly after.

*****

That evening, my mother cooked *waaykye*, my favorite Ghanaian dish. Although she was the queen, she loved to cook for me with her own loving hands. Since I'd returned home after many years, she had the maids prepare other traditional Ghanaian cuisines in addition to celebrate. The elders in the palace among those who lived outside the palace were all invited. For the first time, I came face to face with many of them who all thought I was dead. They welcomed me and thanked the gods for my safe rturn home.

Elder Kofi teased me about how sassy I'd been in my youth. Another elder, who was also a close friend to my father, praised the gods and said it was both a miracle and a blessing that I survived the atrocities, considering that most of the girls my age who escaped the country had been hunted down and killed. While we all ate, they continued to tease me.

"So do you still remember Twi?" Femi questioned teasingly, sitting right beside me while I glared at my friends who sat at the opposite side of the table.

"Oh! Who's that?" Maya asked.

"Not who. It's our native language!" Femi exclaimed, laughing playfully. Everyone at the table exploded with laughter.

After dinner, I proceeded toward my friends' room. I was trying to teach them some basic *Twi* but was having no success. A few minutes later, our laughter was disrupted by a knock at the door. "Yes?" I called out to whoever was there.

The door opened more slowly than usual. When I realized who it was, I immediately got up from the bed and opened the door wider. My dad was standing there, looking somewhat healthier than before, yet still very much unwell. I held his hands and carefully led him to sit on the bed. "I think I know this song," he remarked, waving his arms in a dancing motion.

"Um, I doubt that. People here listen to Cardi B?" Adelaide asked, looking at me in surprise.

"Carly, who?"

"Caaarrddiii B," Adelaide emphasized.

"Oh well, yeah, no! But I do like the beat. It's nice," he replied.

I could see his hands were shaking, and his lips were trembling. He was struggling with every word he spoke. "You don't look so well, Pa. You should rest," I said, placing my right hand on his shoulder. From the corner of my eyes, I could see the growing con-cerns on my friends faces. They were filled with empathy.

Voice shaking, my father responded, "Ah, rest is for the weak. We have much to do before I give you the throne."

An awkward moment of silence followed his statement. I got up and held his arm as we made our way out of the room. I knew they were just as confused by what father said and yet understood very well what he was implying. We quickly reached his bedroom, which was just down the corridor. I requested he stop speaking and lie down immediately. Acting upon my request, he got into bed but could not close his eyes. The conflicts in his mind constantly harassed him. As I switched off the lights, I saw him closing his eyes.

Leaving his bedroom, I quietly shut the door behind me. Seeing him this way had exhausted me. Too tired to return to my friends, I went to my bedroom instead. Before I knew it, I had collapsed onto my bed and fallen asleep.

At the break of dawn, I opened my eyes, but I was too tired to get out of bed. Focused on what my Father had said, worried thoughts still filled my mind. Without changing out of my sleeping wear, I rushed to my father's room. I opened his door slowly and carefully. Once inside, I jumped on his bed, positioning myself right beside him.

"Morning! Pa, how are you feeling? We have a lot to do today so you need to get up," I said excitedly but received no response. "Pa?" I shook him. I must have shaken his shoulders for at least five long minutes. But it was no use. He didn't respond. His body had no pulse; his eyes were completely shut. "Pa!" I held his face in my hands and kissed his forehead. As my eyes swelled with tears, I realized what had happened. My father, the king, was dead!

Pain and anger blinded me, and suddenly I couldn't see him anymore. I darted out of the room, rushed downstairs, and staggered into the garden just to breathe again. I saw my mother standing in front of the garden watering her flowers with her back toward me. Feeling a lump in my throat, I couldn't get any words out of my mouth. Instead, I reached out my hand and tapped on her shoulder. "Mum," I whispered faintly.

"Asha! Are you crying? What is wrong?" She was startled. Both by the way I had approached her and my unusual outburst of tears.

"Pa, he's not moving."
The world came crashing down on my mother. I couldn't utter any more words. She understood what had happened.

A maid had just arrived and was standing beside us. She overheard the conversation. My mum instructed her on what to do and she sped off to notify the rest of the palace about the tragic news. My mother and I went upstairs to my father's room. Femi was already sitting beside his bed. His head buried in the bedsheets.

He got up, revealing a face covered in tears, and hugged my mother. Moments later, my friends appeared in the doorway, waiting for an invitation.

Femi politely invited them in. "Today, she will need all the support you can give her," he stated.

It is a devastating day.

*****

The funeral was scheduled for the following week, and just three days before the service, the elders spoke of an ancient ritual. This ceremony was beyond my understanding because it seemed brutally pointless to me. It involved the forceful kidnapping and sacrifice of three young virgins. According to this ritual, the young maidens' blood would guarantee the king's passage to heaven and provide a smooth journey. The thought of this madness tormented me. Innocent lives being taken for someone who was already dead? I absolutely was not in support of it even if that person was my father. I spoke up against this ridiculous practice when I approached my mother. "Mum, I need to talk to you."

"Yes?" She was standing alone in the garden's corner.

"This is not right. Pa would have never let it happen."

"Let what happen?"

"The bloody ritual. How can innocent blood serve as a pathway to heaven? You need to stop this!" I implored my mother.

"Really? Have you forgotten your traditions so soon? Besides, it's out of my hands. It's Femi's decision."

I was surprised and disappointed that my brother would even consider such a thing. I considered gathering all the elders in my father's study, but that wasn't enough. I gathered everyone who mattered within the community.

At my request, they all assembled in the garden the following day. I pleaded with them. "You're all aware my father just passed. He was an advocate and believer in peace and freedom. He always spoke up against cruelty and injustice. As you all know, my brother Femi will be the successor of the Ashanti throne.

However, this idea of the burial passage rite must remain in the past. My father, your king, would never approved of this. He used to think with a clear mind and a kind heart and always said, 'A country that doesn't adapt to its environment and change does not grow.' I suggest we immediately put an end to this old outdated ritual. The women in our community deserve better."

To my surprise, most of those in attendance agreed with my thoughts. Femi's decision was rendered void. From the corner of my eye I could see Femi standing amongst the crowd of elders and my friends standing right next to him. I could tell from his face he wasn't particularly happy with me. My prescence in the palace was already unraveling things. Even though he was my brother, he was the successor of my father's throne—meaning as the soon-to-be king, his status was well above mine. But I honestly didn't care enough to consider that. Forgivable though his arrogance and pride may have been, I didn't see how he could be so insensitive towards women and so unconcerned about their lives.

I had an inkling what I had done would cause tension between us. In my defense, I knew what it was like to be haunted by old traditions and prophecies. It almost cost me my life. The very thought of my family being part of something like this made me sick. From afar, I felt the anger Femi had for me, and I knew our relationship had developed a barrier that wouldn't be resolved easily.

The Birthmark

"A weeklong funeral and festivities? Are you serious? Is it the mourning that lasts for a week or—"

"It's everything. There will be other events Adelaide. Funerals here are a big deal. It's not a one-day thing. And this is a king's funeral we're talking about," I explained.

"But feasts and dancing, though?"

I nodded my head. "Yes."

Jay stared at me for a moment, then addressed Adelaide and "Hey, guys could you give us a moment?"

A look of worry flashed across Adelaide's face as she looked at him"Is everything all right?"

He looked worried. He was now pacinback and forth. I could tell he was anxious.

"Let's go Adelaide," Maya puld her by the arms.

Immediately after the door closed, He moved toward me and hugged me. I gave in and hugged him back. We held each other for a few moments, enjoying the warmth of each other's bodies. "What's up, babe?" I asked him, unable to control my smile.

"Look, I know things has been pretty crazy,"
"Yes?" I asked quizzically.
"You know I'm here for you, right? No matter what."
"Yes, of course, I do."

"With everything happening, it makes me think—you know, about us. What if they choose you as the queen? What will you do? What will it mean for us?"

I paused for a moment, not knowing what to make of it. "Look, Lani, my brother is the next ruler. End of the story. We'll be heading back to the States after the stupid ritual confirmation and the coronation. Relax, all right?"

"Birthmark confirmation?"

"Yeah, supposedly, the next ruler will have some birthmark legitimizing their rule."

"And your brother has this?"

"Yeah, I mean, he *should* have it."

"Have you seen it?"

"No, but it's not for the naked eyes. There's a reason only the priest and elders do this ritual."

"So he may not have it."

"That's not a possibility. Every legitmate ruler has it.

"Okay, well if you're sure then I'll leave it be. I just want to make sure you're okay, and it's understandable if you're not."

I smiled "I'm fine. It's just that everything's happening so fast you know. It's just a lot to take in."

I drew my strength from my father. He raised me to face adversities with courage, and today wasn't the day to be weak. I had become the glue that held the palace together and everyone was aware of this. "I love your strength." Jay said and kissed my forehead.

His stress may have been relieved, but mine had not. All the questions he brought up hunted my mind. I knew my sense of calmness was a mask; I was lying to him. I couldn't figure out why I didn't just burst into tears as my entire body was begging me to do because the sickness in my gut was getting worse each day.

Maybe it was my nerves getting the best of me. Or perhaps it was the truth.

*****

The day of the funeral finally arrived. The palace had been decorated and staged for the funeral. With the absence of joy, everything seemed gloomy. A large black cloth hung outside the palace indicating grief. Everyone wore either black or red. Culturally, the black and red colors worn for funerals signifies a grieving period. People had come from all over the world to pay their respects—monarchs, tribal elders, politicians, celebrities, relatives, elders, and generals. Some were here for genuine reasons and others to further their ow agendas.

People looked at me in awe, filled with questions and concerns that I was still alive after all these years. Many of the elders, council members, and people who lived through the tragedies that sent me away all assumed I was dead. That was the story my family told everyone. Only a select few elders within the palace knew the truth about my whereabout. They swore to keep silent or my father would have had their heads. So I can imagine the questions that filled most of their heads as I swayed gracefully on the arms of my brother and mothers arms.

Everything was a little over the top as far as I was concerned. The coffin was fashioned with gold, diamonds, and other exotic jewels adorning it. Also, to my disapproval, Femi had decided to go through another one of the old traditions of putting gold, rhinestones, jewels, and other valuables inside the coffin. "Have you not insulted my customs and history enough?" Femi snapped at me when I tried talking him out of it.

"Your customs? Last I checked I was Ghanaian," I snapped back.

"Leave him be. That's what your father would've wanted. Besides, I'm sure he's still upset about the stunt you pulled with the elders. He needs to prove to them he understands our traditions well enough to lead. It's not about you." My mother assured me.

It was an emotional day. People paid their respects through gifts and tears, and some even shared a few words in our native language. I was next in line after my brother to share a few words. I walked up to the podium, feeling the crowd's weight behind me, with a speech in my hand.

I cleared my throat and looked over at the crowd. Hundreds of people were watching me anxiously and waiting for me to speak as if I had the magical words to reverse the grief and pain the country was facing. I couldn't wait to be done and get to the celebration of his life and reign. Ghanaians believed that the last day of a funeral, usually Sunday, is a time to celebrate the life the of the. He was loved. I took a deep breath and began reading a few words. "My father was a great man..." before I could finish a giant lump formed in my throat. The tears I had been holding in all this time dropped from my eyes, and I choked. It was all just too much for me. I sobbed as my mother walked me down from the stage.

I ran up the stairs and into my room. I locked the door and sobbed even harder. *It was my father's funeral, and I couldn't even pay my last respects to him.* I thought, *What sort of daughter am I?* A question I was convinced everyone else was wondering about me. My head sank into my arms and I continued to cry. There was a gentle knock on the door.

"It's me. I'm alone."

"Go away. I just need a moment." I responded. I tried to stop my tears as hard as I could. I rarely cried in front of others no matter how close they were to me. But today, I failed.

"It's all right, Asha. It's okay. Open the door."

I hurriedly wiped the tears off my face and let him in. Jelani stood there with a bottle of liquor and two glasses. "It's been a long time, hasn't it?" he said, cocking his head at the liquor bottle.

"Lani," I started and stopped almost immediately, tears welling in my eyes once again.

He nodded and set the liquor bottle down on my nightstand. Then he pulled me into his chest and gently rubbed my head. "Asha, You are one of the most challenging people I've ever met. You clawed and nailed your way to where you are now. You had to fight your way through everything. That says something doesn't it? And I'll be the first to say that you deserve it. You may be an officer and a princess, but you're still human and a daughter."

I nuzzled against his cozy body. "It's more than just that Jay."

"Maybe so, but I wasn't finished. The burial has been delayed. Your old man's here. Your brother had him brought over so you could pay your final respects without all the tension."

"What? He did that?" I asked, intrigued, and surprised. "Yes, so hurry and let's go. The entire burial is delayed because of you."

"So what did you bring this for?" I asked, hinting at the alcohol.

"For you, fool! A little now and a lot more later." he said before handing me the bottle." He winked. "Now, let's go."

We walked into my father's room. Before me was my father— the man I had loved my entire life. "I'll be outside," Jay said and walked out.

I slowly made my way to the coffin with tears in my eyes. "Papa!" I finally cried out. Although it had been so long since I'd been gone, our bond had always been unbreakable. "I love you," I said with tear-filled eyes. "I wish we would have had more time. I do. You don't understand how much I regret being gone for so long and allowing you to convince me to stay there. I know how much pain that must've caused you."

That day, I cried like I never had before. Not even my violent childhood trauma warranted this many tears. As I left the room, a sense of emptiness filled me. I took all my emotions, pushed them aside, and walked outside to join my family for the burial.

*****

The next day, the celebration started. It had been a hard week for me but I was determined to persevere and pull through it. Rumors about a new king had begun circulating the palace. Who would be the king's successor? When will he be crowned?

My mother was getting the same nagging feeling that I was having.

"Be prepared," she had told me on the last day of the festival.

Why were we all so unsure of what was happening? Was it instinct? What was it? I convinced myself it was all in my head, so I didn't bother bringing it up. The last thing they needed was something else to stress about.

As for my mum, I asumed she was just tensed about the death of her husband. Despite her anxious state, she was still abe to prepare Femi for the ritual. I decided to take my mind off it. I sat on my bed, replying to all of my emails and messages. Some were friends and colleagues back in the States who were oblivious to the events taking place here. "*They do not understand,*" I said to myself.

Suddenly, there was a knock on my door. "Come in," I said, quickly replying to the last of my e-mails and closed the laptop.

There stood Femi. I felt like punching him in the face. It took every ounce of restraint within me not to take a sharp jibe at him when I remembered his behavior toward me when I questioned him about the excessive decorations on the coffin for our father. "Yes?"

"I'm sorry. I didn't mean to talk to you that way."

"Are you sorry for the way you said it or what you said?"

"Both! There is the burden of an entire nation on my shoulders," he said and sat down. "I have never done this before, Asha. I'm under a lot of stress. It may be hard for you to understand." He added, leaning back into my bed.

I debated whether it was even worth continuing to fight with him. I decided to let things go. He was my brother, after all. "Femi, relax. Politics is in your genes. You were born for this. You learned a lot from Dad. You're prepared! Relax. You'll be fine."

I told him and I laid next to him.

"I know, but one simple mistake and the consequences could be devastating."

I sighed and shook my head. Why was he so worried? He was about to be crowned king. He needed to be happy and remain calm. I had to comfort him. "Look, I know what you mean. When I joined the navy, it was new to me. I had to walk on eggshells for months until I figured out a way to tailor it to who I am. So trust me, I know what you mean. Understand that your nerves are only temporary, and you'll get your shit together sooner than you think."

"Why do you keep cusing? Don't let Mum hear you."

"Ah, leave Mum to me. My point is you'll get through to it. Try not to think about it too much, alright?"

"It's harder than you think."

Femi seemed to feel much better after we talked. I opened the door for him as we headed downstairs for lunch. "Thank you," He wishpered.

I acknowledged his remark with a smile.

"I'm not joking, Asha. I will need all the help I can get once I'm crowned."

"I know, but i told you, you'll be fine. Damn!"

"Wow! Again? Mum!" he yelled downstairs.

"You have got to be—" I caught myself and raced down the stairs after him.

"What I meant to say was, will you be my advisor?" he said.

It was sweet of him to ask, but what he was asking was something I couldn't give. I gave him no response and just looked at him. "All right. Tell Mum I will not be joining the table for lunch." He said and marched off.

The high priest, selected elders, and the Kumasi Traditional Council had no issues with Femi being appointed. They just needed to identify the birthmark, so his legitimacy could never be brought into question.

"Here you go." My mother served Adelaide her lunch. She made fried plantains and bean stew.

"I didn't expect this to be so spicy and delicious!" Adelaide remarked as she licked her fingers after going through her first plate.

My mother smiled at her and turned to me. "Where's Femi?"
"Femi?"
I swallowed a morsel of food in my mouth. "He said he didn't feel like eating."
Mother shot a look at the food but spoke no further.
We talked and laughed as we ate. I could tell my mum was upset about Femi's absence. Her husband had just died and her soon and king-to-be son gone rogue. "All right, when you're all done, leave the dishes! The maids will take care of it. Besides, I need to do a little cleaning myself. All of you, to your rooms, please!" she announced halfway through the meal.
Jelani and Maya looked at me. I kicked Adelaide before a single word came out of her slowly opening mouth. "Hey!" she yelled.
She was about to go off on me when I hissed at her, "Let it go." She pouted and looked away. I nodded at Maya. She and the others got up to leave. "Sit in Jay's room for a while. You guys go on! I'll be there in a minute, I need to talk to my mum." I said glaring over at my mother. "

My mother didn't wait long to speak. "Stay here until your brother is crowned king," she told me before I could open my mouth.

I sighed. "Of course, I will. There is no question about it."
"This is a significant event. You cannot miss this for any reason."
"Yes, Ma."
"If you don't attend, the consequences will be immense."
"Yes, Ma! Jeez, give me—"
"Your brother will not take it kindly at all. Your father would've wanted you to attend, and you'll be insulting the family if you don't."
"Mum, I know. I'm going to be here."
"Also, your friends will have to leave."
"Yeah, I know—wait, what?" I questioned.
"They dont value our culture and they don't understand the significance of the rituals in our culture. They fail to respect it. Hence, they will have to leave."

"Mum, please, you can't just—"

I hardly finished my sentence before she interrupted me again. "There will be no arguing with me. They leave, you stay. End of the story," she said as she walked away.

I angrily sighed and shook my head. *I can't catch a break, can I?* "I'm making no promises, Ma! I'll talk to them!" I shouted at her before she turned a corner.

She yelled something back at me but I rushed out of earshot. I couldn't sleep that night. Tomorrow, they were going to confirm Femi as the rightful heir. The ritual had nothing to do with me, yet my mind could not be at ease. I was restless.

The next morning, my mother came and woke me up. "Get up!" she shouted, pulling my sheets off me.

"Mum, I never slept. I'm up," I replied groggily. "Why do you keep treating me like I'm a child? You're acting like a crazy African mum."

"I am a crazy African mum," she said, ignoring my first comment. "We do not have any time for your tantrums. Your brother is already in the room. They have already started the birthmark ritual. Get up! It won't be long before they come out."

"All right, all right!" I said as I got up. I got ready and we both headed downstairs. We were expecting to see Femi outside clutching a body part and wincing in pain but smiling at the same time like the psychopath he was, but he wasn't there.

"He won't be long, surely," my mother said.
I half thought of asking her if I could wake up the others, but I knew it would lead to us arguing so I left it alone.

Half an hour had passed, and we heard grunts and winces from inside the room. The discovery of the birthmark was painful. There were only certain places on your body the birthmark could be found, and let's just say these elders were thorough. An hour passed. The winces and grunts turned into light screams.

Eventually, an hour and a half passed. "Why is he still asking them to continue?" my mother yelled as she overheard him screaming something in our language. Two hours passed away, and now we could hear screams of anguish coming from the room. Another half hour came and went; my mother couldn't take it anymore. She said something in the native language, which I'm sure meant something foul and marched inside the room. She eventually emerged with tears in her eyes. Femi was clutching his body; he was covered in bandages.

"How could they not have found it? How? What is going on, Mother!" Femi was asking frantically.

My jaw dropped as I heard Femi say these words.

"What now?" I asked my mother calmly. I was shaken. *How was this possible?* I wondered with amazement and frustration.

"You! Go inside!" Mother snapped at me.

My heart skipped a beat. "What? This isn't for me. You have to be joking because I'm not going through that," I replied, a sense of dread creeping up on me. *Femi won't allow this.* "Yes, I know he'll stop this."

The elders came outside, all staring at me. One was wiping the blood of my brother from his hands, while the others looked at me as if I had no choice. "You have to!" He hissed.

I tried to keep myself grounded as thousands of possibilities floated in my head. "The only thing I have close to a birthmark is a damn tattoo. *This shit isn't for me*, I thought. I didn't want to put myself through that pain. I was most afraid of them finding something than not. It would complicate everything. "Mum, I'm not doing this. Please don't make me," I begged.

My mom cried. "Yaa, if you don't do this, the throne leaves our family indefinitely."

"And there's no guarantee that it won't even if I do this."

"You owe it to your father to try," she pleaded. "Go inside!"

Femi shouted impatiently, and my heart sank. Tears filled my eyes. The elders dragged me into the room as I yelled, cursed, and cried, resisting. With my head bowed down, I prayed for an intervention.

"Femi! Are you sure you're all right with this!" I shouted, des-perately hoping for him to reconsider. I wanted to make sure he understood the implications of what he was making me do. He was bound to be disappointed.

"Yes!" he shouted back, and I sighed in disappointment as the door shut. I took a deep breath and tried not to think of all the consequences if the birthmark was discovered. Could my father have favored and trusted me to rule over my brother? Could destiny have favored me over my brother? I hoped and prayed desperately that it was not the case.

"We'll start with the back of your ears and move on from there," said one elder.

"You know, back in the States, this is child abuse, or kidnapping. The list goes on," I spat out.

"Good thing we're not in the States," the high priest responded.

"Clearly! Knock yourself out, but please expect a lawsuit." They all laughed at my comment and continued. we'll move on to your shoulders."

With all the talking, I didn't realize they had even started the process. To distract myself, I looked about the room. It had white floors, gray walls, with a dark gray roof. I felt a stinging pain in my shoulder as the elder struck into my flesh while the others stood around chanting. I looked at the equipment in the room to avoid screaming. They all looked unorthodox and unsanitized. *"Bloody customs!"* I cursed under my breath. Common painkillers weren't even considered to minimize the pain; It supposedly went against the centuries-old ritual. *"the pain is part of the process."* They would say.

That's stupid, That was the part that made this entire ordeal even more impossible to endure. As I felt the knife sliding under my skin, I gritted my teeth. Then suddenly, the chanting stopped. The knife stopped moving, and the priest stopped pacing. It was completely quiet. "Okay, what's happening? Can I go? Are you done?" I asked them, but there was no response. "Hello?"

"Shhh," someone responded.

I laid there in silence anxiously until finally an elder yelled, "Impossible."

Another one whispered, "We've found it! We've found the birthmark and our new ruler."

The Stolen

The moment I heard the elder gasp, "Impossible," the bad feeling I had been having in my gut all week settled more deeply into my stomach. The words they spoke made the pain I was feeling even more detrimental. I've never felt so much physical trauma. I felt my life slipping away as I allowed myself to merge with nausea allowing it to take over.

Suddenly, not breathing was a lot more bearable than fighting. I had allowed my tradition to force my death. *My father would be proud of me. At least I tried*, I thought.

As I fell unconscious, my subconscious mind reconnected me with my father. He wrapped his arms around me and hugged me and tears fell from my eyes. I was convinced my death had arrived. "What are you doing here?" he said. Tears continued to flow from my eyes.

"I let them kill me. I knew one day our culture and customs would be the death of me."

"You're not dead," he responded. "But if you give up, you will be. Why do you think I sent for you? Do you think sending you away was eay? You and I both knew this day would come."

"I don't understand. Why would you do this? These people are going to kill me. They will never accept me."

He laughed and shook his head.

"Dad, this isn't funny. If I don't die now, I will soon anyway."

"These are your people, Asha. They will learn to love you, as you will learn to love them. Trust me. This is what our country needs."

"Really, and what about—"

Before I could finish my sentence, I heard my mother's voice from a distance. "Asha! Asha!" I contemplated whether I wanted to respond as I turned to look toward her voice.

"You need to return," my father continued. "Wipe your tears. Queens don't cry. They prevail." And in a matter of seconds, he was gone.

"Asha! Wake up!"

My body felt the aggressive jolt and pressure my mother was using as she shook me. "I'm up! What's going on?" I responded, still unsure of what was happening.

"Hallelujah! Hey! Thank the gods," my mom exclaimed and hugged me.

I looked around the room. "What's going on?" I repeated.

"Well, all that matters now is that you're well. The elders found the birthmark. You're the queen of Asanteman."

I realized I had been dreading ths feeling ever since my father died. His words came back to me: "Queens don't cry. They prevail."

I wanted so much to believe that my father had made a mistake for once in his life and went against nature in making me his heir. But hearing this had been part of a plan from decades ago made me realize there was no way I could have escaped this. He planned this exactly how it was supposed to be, and the gods of our land were allowing it. Who was I to oppose? I had no choice but to prevail. Every decision was part of a bigger plan, and it was always for the god of his people. His rule over the Asanteman was unmatched. I only hoped that he would be here to guide me.

There were two concerns I feared gravely as the next ruler. Firstly, even though women's rights had significantly improved in Ghana, there had only been a handful of female leaders throughout our history and even fewer whose administrations were productive. Dating back to 1900, during the War of the Golden Stool against the British, Nana Yaa Asantewa had been the role model and idol for female leadership and outstanding representation for women empowerment within our society. Since her reign, we had enjoyed some success with modern-day leadership roles, yet nothing that close to her position as the leader of the warriors who stood up against the British colonizers. Though my people had come a long way from there, having a female sovereign was still something I knew they wouldn't react very well to. There had been no record in history sugges-ing that a woman ruler had ever even been considered.

This was a profound event and one that I would spend a lifetime protecting. My father always said that he wanted to make an impact. I never knew he would use the very thing that put me at risk and drove me away from my home to manifest a lifetime of history that not even the gods could unravel. My gender, which once made me a target culturally, was now the very thing thousands of leaders would travel to revel in. I was the first female ruler in the entire African continent.

How do you exist when everything in the universe is against you? I thought of all the obstacles I would face—elders who wanted nothing to do with women in power, those who would specifically dislike me for surviving afterso many had died, citizens who were still accustomed and loyal to old traditions, my contract with the navy back in the States, and lastly, Femi, who would hate me. His eyes was glazed with pain. I'm not sure how he will react once he figured out what has happened.

We never got the opportunity to grow up in the same household, but I still knew him more than he thought. He took his pride seriously. Why else would he have them continue to flay almost his entire body to look for the birthmark. Femi's entire torso had been covered in bandages when he stepped out of the room. Even his upper legs and ankles were not spared. I knew he was going to take this as a blemish to his pride. As the only son and the eldest, it was his birthright he be the next king, and I had stolen it from him.

In some ways, I agreed with him, and I was sure most of my subjects wold as well. I would spend my entire reign convincing them I had just as much right to the throne as my brother. Provoked by my thoughts, I felt the thrill of adrenaline pumping through my blood in response to the cuts made on my body. Or perhaps this was to prepare for the fight I knew lay ahead of me—a war I had waged with everyone I loved.

*****

Today was a day I couldn't afford to be anything less than perfect. Being in the military, you're expected to make little no mistakes. I've seen genuine people make the faintest error, and it cost them their lives. I couldn't imagine both the lives I had now would be filled with politics. Theonly thing I can do, is to do what I have always done to survive—trust my instincts and do my best regardless of the circumstances. I wanted no mistakes or mishaps on my part. I wanted nothing to go wrong because of me.

Today, I would step into the role fate had destined for me and make my father proud. I was saddened. As queen, the little things

I had previously enjoyed—like freedom, the ability to speak freely, the right to dress the way I wanted, and the power to stand by my beliefs—would all end. Not only did I have to prove that being a woman wasn't a disadvantage to the throne for the rest of my life, but I also had to explain and justify the American culture I grew up in and my very existence.

The one thing I was most uncertain about was the reactions of my friends and my boyfriend. To predict how they would feel about all of this was impossible. Although I knew that they would support the choices I made no matter what, this was an entirely different situation; they had their careers to think about. The best I could hope for right now would be their silence to allow me the time to process all this and figure out how best to proceed with my affairs.

Stuck in my own head, I forgot how long I had been lying still on the table. The elders were still whispering amongst themselves. *Queens don't cry. They prevail.* Recalling my father's words, I jumped up to ace my fate. I looked around the room sternly at the elders waiting for them to stop whispering.

One after another, the elders in the room, including the high priest, knelt before me and raised their right hand. With palms and heads down, all pointed in my direction in a gesture of respect and submission. "*Obaahene*," they greeted me, meaning, "Welcome, queen."

Before I could have time to respond, one elder got up. "This is nonsense. We will not have a woman leader," he said as he grabbed his equipment and began to storm out. "The gods of our lands will not allow this. She cannot be our ruler. She barely knows our culture. Kwame, let's go," he shouted as he waved to the others to come along.

"This is an abomination." Elder Kwame, who must've felt pressured stood up.

If any of you wish to be cursed by the gods, follow them! My mother warned them as they started packing up their equipment. I looked at the priest. "I'd rather have a thousand true enemies than one disloyal friend. So, leave now if you must, and no harm will come to you."

To my surprise, no one moved. I was overwhelmed by their trust in me. Not only were they ready to accept me as their leader, but their silence told me they were willing to go against everything they believed in toive me a chance. A queen must never be seen with her head down, so I overcame the urge to return my elders' respect with a deep bow. Instead, I extended both my hands in a palm-down gesture, encompassing all of them, and asked them to rise. Respectfully, they all rose and came forward. "*Me daa se*," I said, patting their backs and shoulders, showing grat-itude for their loyalty.

"Nana, let us clean up your wounds," said Elder Kofi in a concerned voice.

The Ashanti were a tribe of warriors, and knowing this courtesy wouldn't have been offered to a man, as it's considered a sign of weakness to cover up battle scars, I would not have them do so. I could not. "No, let it be, Elder Kofi."

He looked up in surprise at my stern tone, and then with pride in his eyes, he spun to open the doors.

*****

Taking a deep breath, I turned to face my people. As the door opened, I heard the royal messenger announcing throughout the palace, "Let those who have ears hear." *Ding!* "Asanteman has a new ruler." *Ding!* "Asanteman has a new king." *Ding!* "Our king is a queen." *Ding!*

As he spoke the words, people crawled out of their houses, huts, and tents and migrated toward the palace. With the priest in front of me, my mother beside me, and the elders behind me, I walked out to meet my people.

To my surprise, Femi was amongst the crowd. Regardless of our differences, he had always been one of the few people I could speak freely with. To think that had changed now was heartbreaking. I wanted to hug him, but I also knew as queen, tradition forbade me from doing so. At least publically. Althugh I'm not entirely sure I would have either way. He had his pride, but it was nothing compared to the pride of a queen. So instead, I continued to stare at my brother, and like all the elders had done in the room before, he understood what he had to do. Even if he hated me, he respected our family name too much to react publicly. So for now, he had no choice but to control his pride and kneel with the rest of the crowd.

I nodded toward him and patted his back in acceptance. Then with a hand pressed to his shoulder, I indicated for him to get up. As he got up, we came face-to-face with each other. Looking into my eyes, his face crumpled with despair. Without saying a word to our mother or me, he just dragged himself up and shuffled off. My mother looked at him in disbelief. I asked Elder Kofi to send a healer to his room to take care of him and I moved ahead toward the door.

My mother cried in anguish as she reached to touch my back. "Ah! Asha, please let me clean and cover this up."

I instantly felt annoyed.

"Would you have said the same to Femi? Mom, you need to understand something. I may be your daughter, but I am also your queen. I'm not your baby girl anymore. Things will have to change. Do not ask me that question again."

I knew my mother was taken aback at my formal tone, yet she nodded her head slightly.

"I will talk with your brother," my mother said to me. "You must forgive him. He's in a lot of pain right now."

I was unsure of what to say. Everything in my body was telling me to go after him and confront him, but I couldn't. I'm not sure why he was upset with me when he was urging me to go into the ritual room. His silent departure spoke a thousand words, and this hurt me even more. I had lost my father, and now the crown had cost me my brother.

Instead of pondering these matters, I faced my three friends. When they got to the bottom of the stairs, the entire congregation stared in their direction. My heart panicked. I had never prepared them for this. I looked at my mother and she immediately knew what I needed her to do.

"Come!" she said.

My friends struggled as my mother motioned for them to hurry and kneel. As they stood up from kneeling, the crowd cheered in celebration.

"I need to freshen up," I said to my elders. "I needed a change of clothes badly."

"Of course! I will send a maid to assist you," Elder Kofi responded in an overzealous tone.

"No, it's fine. I'll get dressed by myself. Just send a maid to let me know when you're done preparing the council for the coronation. "

Even though the public coronation would take place soon, the counsel coronation was a private ceremony that required only the attendance of my family, the priest, and the elders. This was done in haste to ensure the gods accepted the chosen leader before the coronation day and to bestow certain privileges and rights to me. Yet until the public ceremony, I could not wear the crown or sit on the throne by tradition. "Ma, make sure everyone who needs to be here is here. I will not have any more surprises." Nodding toward them, just as I had observed my father do when he was king, I indicated they were free to go.

As they all turned to leave, my mother looked back at me with disapproval written on her face. "Your friends must leave immediately, Asha," she whispered to me.

"Ma, I know. I'll talk to them later! I'm too exhausted to deal with this right now."

"Okay, but you must attend to this as soon as possible. Our culture will not be mocked," she responded in a harsher tone.

"How are they even, you know what—never mind." With frustration, I rolled my eyes and placed both my hands on her shoulders. "You need to relax. We have too much going on to let their presence bother you. We'll figure this out, okay?" I said in a relaxed tone hoping to ease her mind. Regardless of what she thought of them, I needed my friends with me, especially for the next couple of days. So much had been happening, and they were the only people I knew could keep me grounded. .

"Okay, but I still want them gone," she responded and walked away.

Sighing inwardly at her reaction and my predicament, I turned to face my friends. "What happened to you?" Adelaide questioned in disgust. Both Maya and Jay looked at her sternly. "What? I'm just asking a question. She looks crazy."

Maya immediately grabbed my shoulders and spun me around to face her. I groaned in Anguish. "Asha, tell me it is not true. Please tell me it's not what I think it is. How is it even possible?"

I looked at her, Adelaide, then finally at Jelani. "I honestly don't know what the hell is going on," I told them honestly. "I have the same questions you guys have. I'm not sure how any of this is possible or what it means. But let's head upstairs, and I'll explain what I know."

*****

Once we were in my room, I explained everything that had happened since my mother had woken me up that morning. I could see the pain in Jay's face as I told them about being forced to partake in the birthmark ritual and the torture I went through. "How can they do that," Adelaide shouted.

"Yeah? You're going to tell her mother that?" Maya responded.

I finished telling them everything, including the pain Femi had put himself through in hopes of getting the throne and the elders walking out on me. I explained what my new position meant, the responsibilities it came with, and everything else I could remember.

When I was done, I was greeted with silence. "Look, guys, I know it's not a good situation. I don't think it could get any worse, but I have to do this. They will crucify me if I refuse the throne. My country will be in chaos without a ruler. I can't even give the throne back to my brother if I wanted to. Without the mark of legitimacy the priest will never allow it. The only option is for me to leave the country and make my brother an advisor in charge—but only for a short period. I will have to return soon."

I recounted my options as succinctly as possible. Giving them a clearer picture of the situation and how I intended to handle things before they started asking me more questions than i cared to answe. Out of the three, Jay was the one who may understand how grave the situation was. I noticed a curious expression crossed his face. "What?" I questioned.

Instead of responding, he continued to smile. Finally, he said, "I can't believe it. You've always been my queen, and now you're the queen of your people."

"Yeah, this is crazy," Adelaide added.

"I'm so proud of you," Maya joined. "You're going to be great."

"Yea, if they don't kill her first," said Adelaide.

"Really? Why did you have even to go there?" Maya snapped.

"No offense, Adelaide continued, but these people are crazy. I'm all for culture, but her brother hates her, and half the elders don't want her on the throne. What do you think they're going to do to her?"

I knew there was some truth to her concerns because I wondered about them myself. But regardless of how much they hated me or what I stood for, to kill me would start a series of curses I doubt anyone would want upon them. "They wont kill me Adelaide," I assured her.

"Good, because they would have to kill all three of us." Remembering the pressure my mother had been putting on me to get rid of them, I figured this was the right time to let them know they had overstayed their welcome. "Well, actually, my mom wants you guys gone."

"You know that's not happening," Jay immediately countered.

"My mom won't have it, and I don't want to fight with her."

"Well, as the queen you'll have to find a way because there's no way we are leaving you here. We still have another week left of leave. Should anything happen after we leave, we wont be able to live with ourselves."

I knew Jay was right. Besides the fact that they felt responsible for me, our careers were a matter to consider and it was the one thing my mother didn't understand. She would have to because what I needed right now was far more important than what she wanted. I needed her to think them staying was her decision to make. "Okay, so how about this, if the three of you can convince my mum to let you stay at least till after the coronation, then be my guest?"

"That should be easy," Maya said.

"Hello? Have you met her mother?" Adelaide responded sarcastically, and we all burst into laughter. Wasting no more time, I stepped right into the shower without bothering to undress first. The traditional clothes I wore barely covered me. As the hot water hit my scars, I cried and winced in pain.

Maya stepped in the shower to help me clean my wounds. The pain and the events of the last twenty-four hours had finally sunk in, and I broke down in tears. Maya must have been unsure what to do because she paused for a while and suddenly hugged me without saying a single word. I was thankful she understood me that way. There were no words for what I was feeling. Once I felt ready, I finished showering, Maya helped me dress my wounds and we all headed back downstairs.

*****

It was the first act as the new ruler. In my culture, every monarch before the public coronation and ascending to the throne declared one thing that they would do to better our community. It was a task they would accomplish immediately to show their subjects the kind of leadership to expect. "So what are you thinking about doing?" Jay asked.

"Something that has to do with women empowerment," Adelaide said jokingly.

"I know you meant that as a joke, but that's actually what I'm thinking"

The irony of Adelaide's statement warranted laughter from all of us. With concern Maya interjected, "You need to be careful Asha. Your aren't crazy about their women being equal."

Adelaide quickly rebutted. "Honestly, who cares? What's the point of having a female ruler if she doesn't fight for them? I think you should go for it."

"I'm not saying you shouldn't. I'm saying be careful."

"Women have been at an educational disadvantage since I was born. It's time to change that," I added.

"Why does everything have to be about gender? Why can't everyone be happy?" I heard Jay whisper.

I instantly looked at him in disbelief and noticed my two female friends were doing the same. Understanding what the silent stares meant, he smiled. "Okay, relax! It was a joke. Calm down."

"And you chose now to be funny?" I said sucking my teeth and continued. "Anyway, the education system here for women sucks. I want to make some reforms to it. I want my first act as queen to demolish the societal norms that make it impossible for women to be educated. I also want to launch technical and vocational schools in the villages that are miles away from the cities. Some girls aren't allowed to pursue higher education after junior secondary school, as their families would rather benefit from the bride price in marrying them off. The male-to-female ratio in Ghanaian universities is abysmal. Many of the girls-only schools are severely underfunded, making the quality of education extremely poor. Something needs to changed. I want to be the one who sees it through."

"That's so sad," Maya emphasized.

"I know, its heartbreaking." I agreed with her.

"Nana, they are ready for you." A maid walked toward me and bowed as she spoke.

"Wish me luck, guys," I said to the three people who I trusted the most.

"You don't need it. You're going to be great," Maya reassured me.

"Yeah, don't let them intimidate you. This is what your people need." Adelaide added.

Without saying a word I followed the maid as she led me to the throne room. I was anxious. I was nervous about my appearance and about what I was going to say. But most of all, I was worried about who would withhold their loyalty because of my gender.

My mother walked toward me with calm and reassuring words. "I can distinctly recall the day your father stood in this same position," She said. "I should tell you, he was far more nervous than you."

"I doubt it had anything to do with his gender," I replied with in sadness my voice.

"Maybe not, but nervous all the same. You have nothing to prove. You were chosen, just as your father was. He was an admirable ruler, and you will be too," She said as she wiped the tears trickling down her face.

As the maid opened the doors, a silence spread amongst the officials' faces. I stepped into the room, looking around, just as I had seen my father do countless times as a child. I tried to mimic his walk and his expressions as I walked toward the low dais. I wasn't surprised to see most of the room filled with women. After I looked at them for a moment, they all fell to their knees and completed the ritual of recognizing me as their ruler and pledging allegiance to me.

"Thank you. Your support means a lot to me. I trust you will be loyal and honest to your posts and the throne."

"We will!" they replied loud and clear.

"Nana," Elder Kofi began, "you may now deliver your first act of declaration. What issue within our community do you wish to address first?"

With my mind somewhat eased by how smooth things were going, I spoke freely of my intentions. "I want to make education more accessible for the women in our community. I intend to establish vocational and technical institutes that educate women and give them marketable skills to earn their living. If more women started working, it would significantly improve the economy of our country and it decreases the poverty level within our villages.

My speech was given with so much emotion. The level of passion these topics required created a knot in my stomach. The women in the room started clapping, and the men soon followed suit. Yet, I could see the individuals who weren't in sup-port of this.

"Are you out of your mind?" a man from the crowd shouted. "How can you be so naive? We are on the brink of war with several countries, and your first act as queen is to build schools for women? Don't you think your father would've done so if it was necessary? This isn't America. This is Ghana. The issues we face are far too great to be concerned with women's education."

As the man spoke, I noticed I recognized the voice. Of course, it was Femi. He was standing near the doorway. I looked toward him withholding every curse word I wanted to let out.

"No, this isn't America," I said evenly. "But maybe we could learn a thing or two from them. Winning wars is important, but so is educating our women and children. If our economy continues to stagnate, as it has for years, we won't even afford the food we will need to continue fighting. Education is a resource we need. And not just for men. If our ancestors had been educated enough about the resources we possessed, do you honestly think they would've traded with the British? We traded our gold and our people for things like salt and sugar. Without education, we are lost. We cannot fight any wars, let alone win them. We may as well fall to our knees and beg the old colonists to come to our rescue. Does anyone here really want our people to become financially and resourceful dependent again?"

I saw a shadow of panic cross my brother's face, but he continued to glare at me. I didn' know how to resolve this situation in such a public scene. Back in the States, freedom of speech and self-defense were rights women were entitled to. It was a shame my country thought differently. I could not react the way I wanted to. Not as awoman and certainly not as a Queen. I had to resolve Femi's insubordinate attitude soon before things got out of hand. This could never happen again.

The Crowned

Well, that couldn't have gone any better. I thought bitterly.

I was back in my chambers after the whole fiasco, wishing my father was here to guide me. *"You need to handle this!"* I scolded myself. "You can't keep wallowing. Queens don't cry. They prevail."

Letting out a sigh, I decided to take a break from all of this and get some rest. It was our father Femi was really angry with not me. This wa not about me. There was no way in hell I was going to approach my brother about his behavior. He was the one who would have to come to me.

My friends were still struggling to convince my mother to let them stay, but the chances of that were damn near impossible. Some of the most influential elders were still against me, and all I could do at this point was to be the best leader I could. The main issue at hand? I was still a United States sailor. I imagined the uproar my involvement would cause if my people found out, but nothing could compare to the chaos that would surface if my royal identity was revealed to the Americans. To be honest, I had no idea how to proceed.

It had been almost ten hours since the private coronation, and I was waiting to hear from my mother regarding how it had gone with Femi. I was hoping he would pay heed to our mother. I heard a knock on my door and without even bothering to look up I answered, "Come in."

"Nana," the maid began and paused. "Your mother would like to speak to you. She's standing outside."

It was weird to now think my mother had to ask for permission to see me. Maybe that was just something I would have to get used to. "Send her in."

"Asha," my mother said as she entered and sat down across from me, "I just spoke with your brother. You know he's not especially pleased by the turn of events."

"Will he talk to me?" I asked, for the first time allowing the sincerity in my voice to show. I needed the drama between us to be over, but he would have to respect me and my position.

"He will. I think it'd be for the best." she said, her eyes downcast. She knew her request was out of line, and there was no way I would even think about agreeing to it.

I understood that was his condition to speak to me, but I still couldn't abandon my position—my status—just so his ego could be satisfied. "You know I can't do that." To be a little more clear, "I won't do it." She shook her head in approval and I appreciated her for it. We both knew her request was unacceptable. I didn't resent her for that; I was only disappointed.

"Asha, I understand your ruling, and I agree. You need to learn how to handle these situations. You're going to be facing a lot of them in the upcoming years but keep in mind, he is your brother and your blood."

"I know, Mum, but I can't make an exception, not even for him," I insisted.

"I understand," she said and laid her hand lovingly on my head. She got up and kissed my forehead before leaving.

And again, I was left alone with my thoughts. I was just numb to the entire situation. I hoped and prayed that it would resolve itself.

The public coronation was to take place tomorrow and just the though of it made me rather nauseous. I knew the older generations would oppose my education plan and eradicating gender inequality. I could only hope the younger generation was more receptive to change and more aware of the current situation gripping the country. The youth may be willing to give women a chance.

I heard another knock on the door, and I assumed it was my mother again. "Enter."

The same maid opened the door and came in. "Nana, your brother requests to see you."

I wasn't expecting that. Maybe he was trying to make amends. I gave him that opportunity. "Send him in,"

Femi walked in and stood awkwardly for what seems like an eternity. We stared at each other. Finally, he knelt, giving me the traditional greeting. I walked forward and put my hands on his shoulders. When I removed them, he got up and stood there. My mouth became so dry I could barely breathe let alone speak. So, I sat back down on my chair and left him still standing. This is what I wanted. He had taken the first steps, It was my turn. I gestured for the seat next to me while we talked.

I could see he was in pain. "You're settling well into your new position," he said offhandedly. I thought that was a rather lame attempt to start a conversation, but I didn't point that out.

"I don't have much of a choice do I?"

"A queen saying she doesn't have a choice. Perhaps I was wrong," he teased me.

I knew where this conversation was headed; however, I did not try to stop it. I wanted to have this conversation. I was done running away from it. "I remember asking you before going into that room, if this was okay with you, and I also remember your response. So what is the problem? You changed your mind? Now you have an issue with me?"

57

"We don't have to get into this." he began. I agreed because the throne had to stay in the family. Regardless of how upset I am, the throne leaving our family would have been worse." He was now angry.

"Well, your actions have been telling me you either don't think I'm family, or you're insinuating that I'm not fit to lead." My voice rose.

"That's not what I meant, and you know it. Of course, you're family, but be realistic and stop trying to twist the facts. You may have been born here, but you weren't raised here. You know nothing about the country you're trying to lead. There has been no female ruler, and you know our people will never accept you. You're upset with me because everyone walks around you on eggshells but I won't. You and I both know this won't work."

Every word that came out of his mouth infuriated me even more. I couldn't listen to his nonsense, I started shouting. "So to be clear, you're saying I'm not good enough to lead right? Tell me, why are you opposed to women being in charge and being educated? You realize while men are out doing God-knows-what, it's the women who are left with the kids? You were born into royalty. You're supposed to look at the bigger picture. How can you not understand that if the foundation of the society, which is women and children, are not educated, we won't last long in this world?

"You already know just how badly we need to better the economy of this country. We can't afford wars, and we can't afford to be divided. Can you not see it, brother?" I implored him. "If we don't do this it's going to hurt us in the long run. You'd win the wars, and I know you would. But at what cost? One generation? two generations? maybe three? maybe we'd benefit from war, but what then? You know it's a vicious cycle, don't you? Hard men create good times, good times create weak men, and weak men create hard times."

Femi's expression was utterly lost to me. I wasn't sure what he was thinking, but I knew what I'd said made sense to him. Regardless of his station, we were born with the sentiment "Country before self." So even if we had just faced the greatest injustices that could be imagined, the country still came before his needs. He thought that a great injustice had been done to him and he wasn't wrong, but he still knew that the country came first.

He still didn't answer me. My father once told me that the mark of a good leader is to know when to speak and when to stay quiet. So I kept my mouth shut.

He paused for a moment. "You seem to know what you are doing. I can't argue that. You have just as much of a right to the throne as I do. I know you are going to do right by us my queen."

This was the first time he'd addressed me correctly and for the first time I believed the drama between us to over. The feud between us was over. Hopefully, we can now begin a new chapter together. I wanted to hug him and talk to him just like I did before I was queen, but I hesitated. "Yes," I said shortly and gave him a warm smile. "How are your wounds?"

"They're healing. I don't care about that. I want to talk about the coronation. They have already begun with the decoration of the palace. You should come out. It's lovely."

I understood why he didn't want to talk about his wounds, and I respected that. "I will, in a while. They're going to prepare me on the morning of."

"Are you nervous?" I sensed a legitimate concern in his voice. "What will happen, will happen. I can't do anything to stop that. I'll just have to face it. I just hope my brother will be there with me when I do." I asked, hoping he would say yes.

"He will be there," he said, giving a sly smile. "Don't worry. You are someone I can stand behind and support. Now, if Your Majesty will excuse me, I'll tke my leave."

"Sure, and on your way out, can you please send the maid in?"
He nodded his head and left.

A few moments after he left, the maid knocked and entered.
"Please send Jelani and my two friends in." She left at once. I
needed their company. They were the only ones to whom I was
not a queen. To them I was just me—Asha.

After a few moments, I heard a knock on my door. "Nana,
they're here."

Oh, my gawd! I thought. *What's with these etiquettes?
Couldn't they just come in without someone informing me of their
presence?* This wasn't going to change, so it's best to get used to it.
"Send them in, please," I said, barely masking my annoyance.

As they entered my heart leaped with joy. *Finally!* I thought.
Someone I can be normal with. I ran forward and hugged all of
them. I was doing a surprisingly good job of keeping it together up
until this point.

"You look happy," Adelaide said.
"You seem surprised." I knew what she was getting at. Now that I
had handled my brother, I felt I could relax a little more.

"Uh, duh! You are about to be crowned queen here!" she said.

Though I couldn't fault my friends for not being accustomed
to our traditions, Adelaide's oblivious personality, which I
loved, needed to be contained. the palace would force my hand
to punish her should they overhear the tone she used to speak with
me. "My homeland. My people. My responsibility. I was chosen for
this by my father. It's an honor, not a death sentence. If you can't
understand that, then why are you even here?" I said, being
completely impartial.

"Okay, so, guys, maybe we should cool it down a bit? Yeah? Like
maybe about fifty percent?" Maya said with a nervous giggle. She
always knew what to say.

"Yeah, I didn't mean it like that. I'm sorry." Adelaide looked at her shoes. "I am."

"Yeah, it's okay," I said. "It's just that things are different. You understand, right?"

"So, Asha, what's going on?" Jay interrupted, clearly eager to change the topic.

"Yeah, what's going on?" Adelaide repeated with a friendly gesture.

"Well, my coronation is going to take place tomorrow, so I'll be busy the whole day tomorrow with the preparations. I wanted to see you guys and ask if you talked to my mum."

"Well, we did," Maya said timidly and stopped talking. It made me assume the worst outcome—probably the only outcome.

"She told you guys to go back, didn't she?" I asked with a sinking feeling in my gut.

"Asha, it's going to be all right," Jay said, putting his arm around me. I looked down, and the tears I had been holding in were on the edge of escaping. I needed to keep them in longer.

"Yeah, Asha, we know you can handle it," Maya said with complete confidence.

Wait, if that were the case, Maya would be the first to cry. Okay, something seemed off. "Hold on, you guys are joking, right? You're lying?" I asked

"Yep," Jay said, laughing out loud. "Babe, we're here with you no matter what."

"Why would you guys do that!" I shouted but laughed at the same time.

"Well, consider this payback for not telling us you were the freaking princess all those years," "You couldn't leak out a few tear, could you?" She turned toward Maya exasperated.

"Of course, I couldn't. I'm so happy," she said with a sarcastic hint of remorse in her voice, and I laughed even more.

"Okay, now tell us what will happen at the coronation, and what kind of security is in place? You're going to be safe, right?" Adelaide said, leading me by my hand toward the bed.

could sit down. Of course, she would be one concerned about the logistics.

"There will be plenty of security. Don't worry. My warriors have already accepted me as their queen, and they will die before letting anything happen to me." Adelaide didn't seem convinced by my assurance. "Look, it works different over here. Since birth, we have it instilled in us to never to break our word. We are loyal to our country, and as it stands, I am the country. They will protect me with their lives.

As I explained things to her, I hoped she would understand a little bit more. "Okay, I'm not saying that they won't be able to protect you. I know they will. But for our sake, can we also be the ones who are assigned specifically to you?"

"I would like nothing more than to have you guys there," I said with sincerity, "but I know my people won't stand for it. There are traditions already being pushed to their limits."

Adelaide nodded; she knew that was coming, but she also had to ask. "What about coming back to the States with us?" Jay asked in a low voice.

I was already dreading this conversation because I didn't quiet figured out what I would do regarding that issue. Leaving the military was more complicated than being crowned. "I don't know about that. I suppose I'll have to go back at some point. I must leave my brother and mother in charge of everything over here." I didn't mention what I would do once I got there, but I knew I would have to figure it out.

"Okay, we'll figure it out," Jay said, shooting a look to Adelaide, who looked like she was about to say something, but stayed quiet. I was glad my mother had allowed them to stay here. For a moment, I could be normal, smile and laugh. After hanging out for a feew more hours, I asked my friends to leave so I could rest.

That night, I slept patchily. I kept having dreams that my people were revolting against me. I somehow ended up on a cliff facing thir an anger. My dreams woke me up at dawn, covered in a cold sweat. Today, I would be facing thousands of people, and it was usually a good omen when leaders had dreams, but maybe not this one.

I realized someone was knocking at the door. God, that knock was getting annoying! I shouted for the person to enter."

A maid came in with my breakfast in hand. "Nana, it's time for you to get ready. You have a lot to go through today." She walked forward and put my breakfast on the side table and handed me freshly squeezed mango juice.

I quickly finished my breakfast, took a shower and put on my traditional clothes for the ceremony. Today was going to be a tiring day. I would have to give a speech and go on a tour of all the important sites. Which was supposed to bring me blessings from the gods. The traditional clothes covered just my chest, and another piece of cloth wrapped around me from my waist to my midthigh. I wore our traditional headband, huge beaded necklaces, waist beads, ankle beads, and bracelets for my upper arms and wrists. My clothes were predominantly yellow with slight streaks of vibrant colors that blended in with each other. The clothing was made of fine linen, and it felt light on me. My hair into six large parts— Bantu knots—and decorated with traditional beads.

I had never had this hairstyle before, but she suggested it would suit me. After they had gotten me dressedanother woman came in and decorated my entire face, shoulders, back, thighs, and feet with our traditional marking. It was the tribal symbol of the Ashanti region. All of this took about three hours, including soaking my feet in spiritual water drawn from our village's well. They say it's strengthening one's feet and guide one's footsteps. I had henna painted all over my feet you could barely see my feet. I was then escorted out of my room into the grand hall from which I was taken out to meet with the public.

*****

When I realized how I would be traveling through the city, I was in awe. I was to be paraded around the city in a palanquin carried by my warriors. I was guided to the stool by my maidens. To my surprise, the seat was comfortable to sit on as the men carried me on their shoulders and walked. I cast my eyes amongst the crowd. I did the royal wave and danced our traditional Adwoa dance while seated. I tried to find my friends but I couldn't see them. I then understood that even though my mother had allowed them to stay for my coronation, they still weren't allowed to take part in it. That struck a nerve but I didn't dwell on it.

After a couple of hours of being paraded through the city and doing uneventful things like having to stop at the shrine to meet with the high priest and atone for the sins of my people—beseech the gods to favor us among all other nations—I heard something that caught my attention as we headed back. "We are doomed. She won't be able to lead us."

"What are you talking about?"
I turned around and saw the two women, both looked in their late thirties. They were discussing me right in my prescence. I stopped where I was standing and faced the people and pretended to be smiling, waving. "She is a woman. She cannot lead a nation of men."

"She is perfect. Did you not listen to the speech she made about women's education? Finally, someone who will fight for us."

"It remains. She is a woman."
I turned around and went into the shrine. It saddened me to believe this was going to be my life now. I would be the subject of people's speculation! Always! If that was the case, so be it. *I'm going to prove them all wrong*, I thought.

64

The Recall

I was lying in my bed thinking over the conversation I heard outside the shrine. I was still trying to wrap my head around it. How could two people brought up in the same environment, the same country, have such wildly different views? It was crazy to me. It was almost surreal to hear them talking about me. Why did people think because you become public figure you stop being human? Do you stop having feelings?

I was stunned, but I reminded myself that this was my life now. Always being subjected to the people's opinion and ultimate belief that I could have done more. That I wasn't enough. They didn't know the entire story, and I wasn't in any position to explain myself to anyone. Just as my thoughts faded away, I heard a knock on my door. I was honestly too tired to even respond.

The maid popped her head in. I shot a glance up at her, and noticed she looked a bit worried. But before I could say anything, she began, "Your friends are here to see you, Nana."

"What's wrong with you?" I asked.
"I beg your pardon, Your Majesty?"

"You look worried. Is everything okay?" I asked again.
"Your friends, they look worried. I think something's happened. Today has been a long day and I'm wondering if youre up for it."

This was someone I'd known since my childhood, so I understood why she was concerned. I grew up playing with them. They were the ones who taught me how things were done in the palae. They all held a special place in my heart. Ever since my father had passed, they have an immense help and I appreciated them.

"Come here, Sit down." I said, patting the bed. "Ada, you've been in my life since I was born, so I appreciate you. But it's going to be okay. You need not worry about me. You don't have to protect me." I gave her a warm smile. "When you're in a leadership position, it's no longer about you. Your subjects come before you. People thought being in a position of power was easy.

" They failed to understand it came with a price that only a few could handle. Our life was always on display, and our actions judged continuously. We needed to be stronger than everybody else.

"I understand, Nana,"
"Now, send them in please."
"Yes," she said and left the room.
I was curious to find out what this could've about.

My friends entered the room wth a panicked an worried look. They must have run to my room. "Guys, what's wrong?"

"There was an intel attack back in the States," Adelaide said in a hurry. "We have been called back."

"Wait, what?" I began pacing. "Intel attack? Seriously? I can't catch a break, can I?" The timing couldn't have been worse.

"Yes, the DC headquarters. Breeden wants all of us back to handle things immediately. Jay said in a much calmer voice. Jay was trying not to panic, and considering what had just happened, I did not understand how he managed that.

I thought my identity was still safe but was that misguided? With the news of my father dying and my being broadcasted all over the world, there was no way of telling who knew what. My superiors in the States might have already found out. There was no way my traditional clothes and makeup would be enough to hide who I was.

What the hell was I thinking? I was trying to convince myself that my true identity was still protected. The timing of this was too convenient not to be considered. How was it possible that barely a day after my coronation, something came up that required my immediate return? Someone attacking our intel systems and software on this day didn't seem like a coincidence. "Wait a minute," I said, keeping a low voice. "It seems convenient, don't you think? All this happening today of all days."

"What are you trying to say Asha?" Adelaide said, her voice rising a bit. "That Breeden was lying?"

Maya and Jay both tried to silence her but didnt succeed. I stood up. "Adelaide, now is not the time for your tantrums. You need to calm down."

"She's right, but everybody needs to relax," Maya said harshly, looking at all of us.

"I'm not trying to say anything. I think it's too big of a coincidence for all of this to happen today of all days. We've been here for almost two weeks now. Why today? Tell me that doesn't sound suspicious."

"Please tell me, I'm I crazy?"

Adelaide took a deep breath, "Breeden wouldn't lie about this. You know how much he's done for us."

"Babe, it seemed true," said Jay. "And honestly, you are one of the best officers they have, if not the best. It would be logical to call you in now. I don't think Breeden would do that. He loves you."

I noticed the sincerity in his tone, but his expression still made me nervous. "Can you guys please give us a few moments?" I looked at Adelaide and Maya.

"Sure," Maya said tugging at Adelaide's arm to follow her out of the room.

"Jay, you know this is a big deal. I can't just up and leave. " I said in a low voice as soon as I knew they were out of earshot.

"I know, Asha. But you're still in the military. Your options here are limted. It's not like you have a choice. If you go, there's a chance that what you're thinking might be true, but if you don't go, you're going to jeopardize more than you can afford. The chances are they find out anyway, not to mention the number of issues your absence will bring between the two countries." He plopped on my bed.

I knew my military status and the recent change in my royal title was a big deal. I didn't know how or when I would handle it, but even as he spoke, a plan was forming in the back of my mind, one that might work. "The thought of leaving so suddenly after my coronation is nerve-racking. Although things are good with my brother, I'm especially concerned about how people react to this news, especially the elders—not to mention my mom. I mean, what plausible explanation could I give to help them understand and accept the terms of my contract and the demands?

"There's no way I could bring myself toexplain to the elders that in fleeing to the States because of the war left a great sense of gratitude from me so much so, I joined their military. In their eyes, the people made up of that institution are responsible for slavery that brought about broken families, death, oppression, and countless Africans' massacred. How could I ever justify being part of it? They would never understand. But there *is* something we can do," I intoned.

"You're the one to come up with a plan," Jay said, smiling.

"Don't get too excited!" I said. "It's horrible, but it's all I've got. What if I tell Breeden about my actual identity?" The only other option I had was to sit around and wait for the US to find out then deal with the consequences.

"Are you serious?" Jay said, shocked.

I didn't like my idea, but I genuinely didn't have any other viable options. "You said so yourself. They're going to find out soon enough, so why not tell them myself?"

I took a long pause, deciding what to do next. "Look, I don't have to tell them everything, but I could tell them something to the effect where they won't feel like I've been deceitful. I can't have them thinking I'm disloyal. Every single mission involving me will be questioned. I have to do something! Now that things have changed, all I want is to finish my contract and move on smoothly."

Jay loked more toubled than before. "Babe, that's a bad idea." "You're overreacting. You need to come back with us and figure out exactly what happened, and we'll go from there. But you're going to have to do something here. Get things sorted out beofre you to leave." There was a tone of finality in his voice. "Being queen doesn't mean shit if you still can't have your freedom."

He sat on the bed, waiting for an answer. "I think I can convince my brother to step in for me while I'm away. Maybe have my mother support him. I must call a meeting with my elders and have Femi help me convince them." I said and walked toward the door. "Tell Maya and Adelaide about this. I have to go talk to my family."

I walked out of my room and toward the throne room. They had scheduled me to move in there officially later today, but I didn't have the time right now. Now was not the time for them to question me, but I would also have to convince them that my decision was the right one. I asked the guards to get my mother and bother to me. "*lets get this over with.*" I wishpered. As I sat on my throne I though of y father. I missed him dearly.

*****

In a matter of minutes, guards filled the throne room, and I called them to attention and dismissed them. They must have judged by my tone that the matter needed their utmost attention because almost all of them jogged off at once, except a few whose duty was to be in the throne room at all times, but even they needed to step out. I couldn't risk anyone else knowing about this, so I told them to wait outside.

After about five minutes, my mother and brother approached me. At once, I could tell that my mother was about to object to my sitting on the throne without the official ceremony, but I held up my hand so I could speak first. "Something has come up. There's a situation back in the States. I have to return. While I'm away, I'm going to need you." I looked directly at Femi. "I need you to help me handle things here while I'm gone. I'm sure Mom won't mind stepping in if you need it, but I can't convince the elders alone. We have to be a united front on this, and hopefully, with your support, the elders will go a little easy on me because I honestly don't have it in me to debate essecially not with either of you. Are there questions?"

"Nana, slow down. What happened?" Femi said, as my mother seemed taken aback. I had expected this. "Look, there isn't much I can tell you now because I don't even know the tire story. But I have to go," I said.

Femi was about to ask another question, before I interrupted. I know nothing about what happened."

"That was not what I was about to ask, Asha. The timing seems very convenient, don't you think?" he said cautiously. He was concerned every right to. I understood why he had the same reservations s as I did.

"Femi, brother, do you trust me?"

"Yes," he said without missing a heartbeat.

"Then trust that I have already thought about this, and I have no other option other than going. Manage!" I concluded.

"But you cannot go," my mother said, finally recovering from her shock. "You are the queen, Asha. You cannot abandon your people."

"I'm not abandoning them, Mother. Why do you think I'm comfortable doing this? I'm not happy." I was damn near yelling at this point. Without waiting for her to answer, I added, "I know there are people here"—I gestured toward her and Femi—"who can take care of my people. I trust you, I need you to trust me and not question me. There's going to be a meeting with the elders shortly. Can I trust you to back me, Femi?"

"You're going to appoint Mom and me as advisors in your absence, right?" he asked, almost to himself.

"Yes. Can I trust you, Femi?" I asked, stressing just how important this was.

"Yes," he said.

"Mother?" I looked at her, She was looking right at me and said nothing. "Mother!" I snapped at her.

"I suppose. I do trust you, you know," she said.

"Good. Let's go meet the elders," I said.

*****

The meeting with the elders went about as I expected. My Mum and Femi stood by my side as promised. I knew they had reservations about what was going on. "Mom, trust me, everything will be okay," I assured her as we walked back toward my room. "Femi will be here." I knew my mother's concerns were warranted, but I didn't have time to give her the attention she needed. The thought of going back to the States left me nervous. If the attack had been the reason for our return, then I would have a peace of mind, as unfortunate as that may sound, because the alternate outcome for our immediate summons would be disastrous, one I would most likely be destroyed from, not to mention the people involved. Not only was I going to be ruining my career, but I had placed my friends' careers and lives in jeopardy. There was no way I could live with that. I hoped that whatever the attack was, it wasn't something that could destroy the organization I had served since I was nineteen years old. Regardless of being the queen here, America had saved me when I had nowhere to go. When my own people tried to end me. I would forever be indebted, and they deserved the same loyalty I was giving my birth nation.

I recalled one elder heckling me. "My queen, you had been crowned a few hours ago. Imagine the perception people will have if they find out that their newly appointed queen left." He'd specifically stressed the word *queen*, and everyone understood that this situation wouldn't have been nearly as dire if I had been a man. It was as if my leaving had any fucking thing to do with my gender. To them, traditions were already being pushed to their limits; to add this to the already unfavorable situation was too much for them.

"The timing of this sudden need for absence is absurd and speaks a distasteful language to our people," the elders continued. "Imagine what kind of message it sends."

I'd calmly explained, trying not to strangle anyone. "I understand that. However, you couldn't possibly imagine the consequences of this situation if I choose not to return."

"You're a queen. You don't answer to them. They don't own you," Elder Kofi added.

"Well, actually, they do," I yelled, unable to control my annoyance. "Last I checked, my people wanted to kill me, and it was for that reason my father sent me away. Do you honestly think a nation will take in an immigrant without her not feeling like she owe them?" I couldn't think. I knew they had a hand in trocities that drove me away. "I know my duties, and I have accepted them. But make no mistake, this right here, about me needing to go back, is all on you," I concluded, looking at all of them.

Never in a million years did I think the situation that drove me away would still haunt me. I had never cared about who was involved. All I always thought about was why my father tried to protect me from everyone else and why he needed to. I was a little girl who could barely even spell her name. What could I have pos-sibly done to anyone so severely that I had to leave my entire family behind? I always blamed the country itself and never linked my pain to the elders. For this to have come out the way it did surprised me. As I stood there watching them with their heads bowed down, filled with shame, I swallowed the slightly sensitive tears that seemed to make their way down my face.

My heart was hurting. "Elders, understand that if I'm telling you I have to go, then it's a must. The option not to go will be far greater. Trust me."

"She's right," Femi spoke up. "We cannot afford a conflict with America. This is the only option. We are her subjects, and she's our queen. We have to trust her intentions and support what she needs," he said, turning to face the elders.

The elders did not dispute. They stood quietly. I figured that was as good of a response as I could hope for, considering the guilt I had sprayed all over them.

Although I had never consciously blamed them, saying it out loud made me feel better. Since my father wasn't here to explain things to me, and my mother insisted on acting confused and clueless every time I asked her about it, the elders were as close as I was ever going to get. Maybe one day, one of them could tell me what the hell happened that called for first-born daughters of generations of women to be slaughtered. Until I was ready for that conversation, I was going to use their role in this devastating act to bend them to my will any chance I got.

"I believe that settles it," my mother concluded.
"I will leave tomorrow morning. Get my things ready and call my friends to my room."

"We leave tomorrow. Get ready." I told them as soon as they walked in.

The Betrayal

I stood still in front of the mirror, looking at myself and trying to understand why this was happening to me. The voice of my father echoed in my ears. "Because you can handle it."

I still thought it was unfair. *Why couldn't I be with Jay and live my life peacefully?* I wondered why my father decided all this was worth the drama. *Why did he need to make me queen and burden me forever?* Things in Kumasi weren't the same as they were in America. If you were the king or queen, you stayed that way for the rest of your life. Freedom only existed in death.

Admittedly, the position came with many privileges, but I didn't want any of them. Life in the suburbs would have been sufficient for me. A grand purposefor life is overrated. If my father saw the queen in me, that was precisely what I was going to be.

I picked up my phone and called my brother after we met with Breeden. It had gone alot better than I imgained it. The execution of the mission played right into Adelaide's alley, and she was calling the shots even after my adamant opposition on how she intended to approach the situation. So I took matters into my own hands and looped Femi in on what was going on.

According to Adelaide, the only way to stop the intel attack was to physically destroy the campsite the Liberians were using as their operating base. There was a reason most countries tried their best to become allies with the States. The level of technology and resources we had was almost unparalleled. It broke my heart to think this was the only method she could use to salvage the situation.

I couldn't let it happen. "Femi, listen to me," I hissed. "It was Liberia!" I had no time for pleasantries and wanted to get directly to the point.

Just as I expected, he said, "What did they get, and how did they even pull this off?"

"Breeden isn't telling us anything. The thing is, they give this information out on a need-to-know basis. Even my clearance isn't high enough for them to loop me in. So I guess whatever information they have, it must be serious," I told him in a low voice.

"So you don't know what they stole, but there is going to be retaliation, right?" he asked in a matter-of-fact tone.

"Yes, they're going to be attacking the site Liberia is operating from. The issue is, it's right in the middle of the city. Alot of innocent civilians will get hurt. We cant sit by and do nothing. "

"They're going to attack, and there isn't much we can do in this situation except try to mitigate the deaths of the innocent and help them after the attack. Have you tried suggesting a lighter approach, one that doesn't kill civilians?" he asked.

His question was logical. However, that wasn't how things operated over here. "I did. They want to do it their way, and honestly, a part of me understands that the people responsible for this didn't care enough about the possibility of innocent people getting hurt, so why should the US? I just can't allow so many deaths on my conscience, not if I can help it. I'll find out the exact coordinate of the campsite that's being targeted. I'm going to give them to you."

"Your job is to make sure the Liberian president gets it. Make it anonymous. I don't care how you do it. Just make sure he doesn't find out it was from us." I said speaking quickly. "Tell the president that he needs to evacuate those areas immediately and as quietly as possible. If the US finds even a hint of exposure in its operation, it'll set off serious alarms I cannot afford—"

"Won't they be sending in ground troops as well?" Femi interrupted. "I had thought about this, and unfortunately, that was something the Liberians would have to figure out on their own.

"They will be, but the Liberian army can handle that," I said uncertainly. "We need to make sure the casualties are limited. Even if they send in ground troops, they'll have specific targets, and they won't be there for a prolonged amount of time," The intel attack wasn't to be taken lightly, but I couldn't figure out why they were okay killing civilians. *What did they do?* I wasn't opposed to sending in the ground troops, but the civilians were innocent.

"Okay, so how long before I have the location? I think I need to pay a visit to the president myself."

"Wait for my call." I responded in irritation.

"Look, if we leave an anonymous tip, it may take weeks to reach the president's ears, and it is Liberia. They get these kinds of threats all the time, so I think if I deliver it in person, it'll be more impactful," he said.

"Femi, I'm sure it will be more impactful, but I can't have the president knowing about our involvement. I'm not ready to answer the questions that will follow suit." I realized that Femi was probably just going to do what he thought best, regardless of what I said. And since I wasn't there, there wasn't anything I could do.

"Asha, I don't intend to walk into his living room and hadn it to him; the fewer people who know about this, the better. I'll visit him in prvacy. I still have some trusted allies in his government.

"It won't be hard," Femi said confidently.

If anyone could pull it off, Femi could. I couldn't believe just how supportive he was because almost anyone else in his position would have advised me against this. Understandably, Liberia wasn't my country, and I was not responsible for them. However, I hoped that if the situation were reversed, Liberia would be just as supportive of Ghana. There had been so many tragedies in the world, and I, of all people, knew firsthand just how painful it was to go through that. My country had been through famine and tring times before my father came into power. I was determined to do what I could to salvage my continent. I was going to prevail.

*****

Just coming out of the meeting with Breeden, I had planned this plan, and now I had to put it to use. I knew just the person to contact to make it happen. However, I remembered the three people in America who still had the right to know what I was up to. I pulled out my phone again and called Jay. "Hey, honey, can I see you?"

"Oh, you miss me already?"

"Not just you. The girls too," I said, laughing. "Just come over."

"What's in it for me?" he asked.

I hesitated for a moment. "Um...I can cook."

He paused for a moment and, with laughter agreed "Um, yeah, guessII'll take that."

I wasn't required to tell them anything, but I needed their support, and they deserved to know what I was planning to do. I felt so close to them now that they knew everything about my life. I didn't want to go back to keeping secrets and telling lies. "Thank you," I replied, and Jay hung up.

I thought about the conversation I just had with my brother. I didn't have a lot of time before Adelaide started on her mission. I needed to get in contact with someone who could help me get this done. Jay had his destiny written the moment he was born. His entire family was scattered across the military's various branches. His father was a general. I hoped he would have the information I needed. Iwasnt thrilled about having to ask this of me, but I didnt see any option.

Just as I was thinking this, I heard a knock on my door, and my friends entered.

"Let's get straight to it. What did you do?" Adelaide quetioned me

There was no time for pleasantries. I recounted the conversa-tion I'd had with my brother. Jay was already nodding before I began talking. "I suppose you know what I'm going to ask from you," I said, looking at Jay. He nodded.

Maya stood still in disbelief, but I guess Adelaide was still processing the information. "What are you guys talking about?"

"Jay's father is a general. I'm asking him to get the coordinates of the locations."

Before I could even finished talking, Adelaide interrupted me. "Okay, no!" her voice rising alarmingly. "You will not commit treason. You are still a part of the Navy. You can't do this! Are you seriously even considering pulling Jay into your mess?! To commit treason with you? Are you fucking serious?"

She loved me, but she was also blind to all the atrocities that her government committed against foreign civilians in the name of protecting America. I tried to be calm, but her words made me angry the more I listened. Even though Liberia wasn't my country, the consequences of that mission were too serious for me to accept. However, unlike Adelaide, I didn't let my patriotism blind me to injustice. With little thought, I yelled, "You want to question my conscience and loyalty? You're seriously saying you'd rather we kill innocent people who have done nothing wrong than saving their lives?" I labored to keep my voice in check, but the tension in the room had gone up a thousandfold.

"In case you forgot, it was the Liberians who put themselves in this situation, not us. They attacked us! So excuse me if I don't side with criminals and pull my friends in with me," she retorted.

That was it! "You imbecile. You can't keep overlooking and making excuses for your country's atrocities the keep committing against so many innocent people. You can't see the difference between being patriotic and being evil—"

"Asha!" Maya interrupted. "Adelaide, you need to check your-self. You might be in charge of the operation, but she's still your superior officer. I think this is a horrible idea, Asha! It will probably end our careers, yet knowing the number of people who had nothing to do with this attack that will die eats at me. I can't imagine how I'd feel if this was Mexico. With that being said, I will do what I can, but if this blows up, I'll deny my involvement," she said, shutting down the argument between us.

Adelaide rolled her eyes and turned in my direction. "You think I don't understand you. I have my priorities in order. You seem to have forgotten our priorities with the United States. I'm still doing that, even if you're not." She turned around abruptly to leave, but I couldn't let her.

"You can't seem to grasp the reality of the situation, can you?" I said, calming down. Adelaide was a great resource. I didn't want us to be on opposing teams. "All I'm doing is giving the location we will strike so that the civilians who have nothing to do with this can evacuate peacefully."

"You're not even Liberian." she retorted.

"It doesn't matter! I know you won't understand because this is your only home. But think about this: if this were happening to Texas and you could help, would you? Or would you sit by because you're not from that state? Can you say that you're in favor of killing all those people? People who have done nothing and have no say in any of this?"

She stopped with her hand on the handle of the door.

"Adelaide, look, I know these are gray areas we're operating from. We're friends, so if you think my decisions are ones that you can't agree with, then that's fine. If you want to remain my friend, then know that you're going to be operating in gray areas. If you can handle that, then stay. If you walk out that door, then I will know your answer."

Giving her an ultimatum was never my intetions. The more I listended to her speak, I realized it was my only choice.

I nevr planned for her to have to choose between our friendship and her country. My only hope was that she would choose me. I looked at her, and she removed her hand from the door handle, slowly turning back.

"I…" Her voice was caught in her throat. "This is too crazy for me, Asha."

This was the first time I had seen Adelaide teary-eyed, and that was hard to fathom.

"It's just that these gray areas seem to get bigger wth each situatn we find ourselves in. I'm afraid I'm being buried under a mound of secrets. And you're right. This is the only country I know," she said, her eyes downcast.

I walked toward her and hugged her as hard as I could. I knew how much courage it took for her to admit that. In reality, I was still apprehensive about every decision I had ever made in my life. I wondered how my father did it. He must have probably always felt the same way. "I know, love." I hugged her harder. "I don't want you to leave, but if you do, I won't blame you or hold any grudge against you." It was cruel of me to expect that from her, or any of them. I wouldn't know what I would do if I were in her place, but I couldn't let her leave, mainly because I loved her but also because she knew entirely too much about me.

She gently moved my hands from around her and looked at me. "I'm not going anywhere. I'm sorry for getting angry. I know you're right. I don't know how I'm going to do this and still sleep at night." She looked at Jay. "So how long before you can get us those locations?

I could see out of the corner of my eyes that Maya was standing there with tears flowing out of her eyes, so I went over to her and hugged her.

Adelaide followed closely behind and joined in. I can't put into words just how deeply I felt for all of them and how much I hated putting all of them through this. They were gems to me, and it felt like daggers to my heart every time I asked them to compromise their livelihood.

After that touching moment, Jay gently tapped on my arm. "I already have a meeting set up with my dad. I can get you those locations in two or three hours.. I have to leave right now."

He shortly left after and we were left alone. All I wanted to do was close my eyes and sleep the ay off.

I was just about to suggest this when Adelaide's phone rang. She showed us the caller ID. It was Breeden. "Hello, sir," she said and put the phone on speaker.

"I need to see you. Bring Asha with you," His tone suggested it was urgent, and I felt fear spread through my body.

"Yes sir! We'll be there shortly."
Both of them looked at me, and I knew they were thinking the same thing I was.

Adelaide spoke up. "It's probably nothing about you, Asha. Don't worry. We need to go. Maya," she said, hugging her and then heading for the door. I did the same and followed her out.

*****

The car ride to Breeden's office was brief. I thought there would be tension between us since we had fought, but we were both behaving normally. A few minutes later, we were headed straight for Breeden's office.

"Come in."
"Yes, sir," we both said in unison and saluted.
"At ease! "
"What going on?" Adelaide asked.
"We need you both out on the submarines in the Atlantic," Breeden begin. "Here are your deployment orders, and you need to leave the day after tomorrow. We need our best people there and that's the two of you."

"What about Jay and Maya?" Adelaide asked at once.

"Oh, don't worry about them. They are going to be joining you guys soon—in about a week. I need them here to take care of some paperwork after the Liberian mission we have planned."

"Sir?" I said timidly. He rose his eyebrows to my voice without ayisng a word. "Is there any update on the Liberia situation?"

"Yes, there is actually, but it doesn't concern you. Now get going!" he said lightly, and the both of us dismissed ourselves. I wasn't surprised at our sudden need for departure. You'd only just returned and the get deployed again.

I headed back home and found Jay and Maya waiting for me. I immediately asked him for an update. "Did you get the locations?" He handed me a file. I looked and was shocked and appalled at the individuals in support of this mission. I had to get this information to Femi as soon as possible.

I called him at once and told him everything. I let out a sigh of relief when he reassured me things would be taken care of. "By the way I'm going to be deployed to the Atlantic for the next few months, so I'll be gone longer than I initially thought."

"Asha, you need to come back. This was not the plan. I won't be able to hold off the elders for much longer. They aren't asking questions now, but soon they will. What am I supposed to say to them?" he asked.

"Brother, I need you to handle the situation. You're the one in charge., and I need you to do this for me, please."

He was silent on the phone for quite a while before answering, "Okay. I will take care of it. But be back soon. We need you back here," he said.

"I know. Trust me!"

Feeling overwhelmed I hung up the phone. I looked at everyone in the room and felt relieved that I still had my friends. "We should get some sleep Adelaide.

Today's probably our last time getting a goodnight's sleep for a while."

"I agreed." Adelaide said.

*****

"There's been a report of over a hundred victims who has fallen to their deaths because of the attack and still counting. The actual number is still unknown. Many people have been severely wounded, and hospitals are flooded with hundreds of casualties from the attack in Freetown, Liberia."

As I lisened to the new reporter talking, I became numb and transfixed realizing that Femi had betrayed me. Once again!

The Prophecy

It was as if someone had pulled the ground from underneath my feet. *How could Femi do this to me?* I trusted him with my heart, my people, and most of all, my throne. I would never have guessed he'd stoop so low as to allow the death of innocent civilians to get back at me.

My surroundings became blurred, and I stopped listening to the rest of the news. Everyone around me seemed to have a smug, self-satisfied look on their face, except me. Yes, they had accomplished their task, but at what cost? Was there any part of them that felt guilty knowing their mission claimed innocent lives. Our government had a long-standing policy of not negotiating with terrorists, but this was a step above that.

My friends stood beside me, and I wondered what they thought of all this. I'm sure they must have figured out by now that Femi had betrayed me. He delibretely failed to deliver the information I gave him out of spite. His hatred for me clearly was much deper than I assumed.

I went back to my quarters, knowing my friends would trail behind shortly. "Why did he do this?" Jay asked me. He was angry.

I didn't answer him; I couldn't. What was I supposed to say? My brothers betrayal brought on an instant headache? I was sitting on my bed, with my head in my hands, ashamed.

"Jay, I think we need to give her a moment," Maya said timidly.

Femi was the one who betrayed me, but I was the one who had trusted him. The heart of the problem belonged to me. Had I had more sense; I would have known that people do not change. If he had contested my becoming queen once, he would continue to do it again until he got what he wanted.

"Yeah, that's probably for the best," Jay said.I wanted them to stay with me, but I needed to think. I couldn't contact my family while we were still at sea. Certainly not about this situation. All communications were monitored, I couldn't risk being overheard. Imagining what Femi may have done with Kumasi by the time of my return broke my heart. I had about two six more weeks left of this deployement. Until then, I would have to take things one day at a time.

*****

"Mother, you better start talking now!" I said yelled. I'd been silent for far too long, and I was unaware of everything that had been going on in my absence.

"Your brother has been working aggressively since the attack in Liberia. I knew about your plan with him, and I thought he would carry it out, but he didn't. The day of the attack, he rounded up the elders. He led them to falsely believe what happened was because of your lack of care. He told them, 'If she could let this happen to our sister country, then how can we trust her?' He's pressuring them to make him the new Ashantehene. The betrayal of your father has blinded him. He will stop at nothing to get that throne." she said, her eyes low. "I have successfully stopped the elders from relinquishing your throne to him. It outrages the people in your absence. You need to make public appearances. Yo need to fix this. You have to do a lot of damage control."

I had spent each waking moment thinking of ways to regain the trust my people. It was clear trusting Femi was a mistake. It was not a matter of pride anymore; it was plain hatred. I left my mother and went to straight to my room.

Jay and I had taken the first flight to Ghana. He refused to leave my side an I appreciated him for it. Our relationship was the only thing I could count on. By now, Femi would have a fair share of the elders on his side, and I needed to do something that would ensure most of them were in favor of me. As I explained my dilemma to Jay, I felt sorry for myself. "What are you going to do now?"

"Simple. I need to campaign and get them on my side. I need to make sure I fulfill the promise I made to my people. Making education a priority for women like I promised. We'll see what happens then." I got quiet, thinking if I should say what I wanted to next.

"What is it, babe?" Jay asked. "Just tell me."
"I was thinking about inviting over the Liberian president for tea or whatever. I'm sure a conversation between us is long overdue."

"That sounds good. You need to make up for the attack. Also, this could be a perfect chance for you to strengthen ties with Liberia." Jay replied.

I needed to think about the campaign that would eventually lead me to my victory. Aside from that, all I had to do was have the palace prepared for the president visit.

Before the day was over, I had already informed the elders about the meeting I had planned. I knew they were expecting to be addressed. Thinking of what I was going to say tomorrow, I tried to sleep. Even my sleep wasn't without its hardships. I kept having nightmares about my brother stabbing me to death and then becoming king. Something my mother had said terrified me more than I cared to admit: "He will stop at nothing." I would like to have thought he would never kill me, but I had seen too much of the world and knew it was a genuine possibility.

*****

The next morning, I woke up in a cold sweat and realized that I had the meeting in three hours. There were still many things to prepare for. My maids helped me get dresed nd shortly after, I was prepare to address them. I probably should have written some speech to give, but I didn't have the time. To be frank, I preferred to speak from my heart.

A ball of nerves overtook me. "I want to apologize for my prolonged absence."

"Do you know how many people want you off the throne?" one elder shouted.

"I will not be interrupted when I am speaking! I know you all have a lot of questions and a lot of things you would like to say, but we don't have time for that." I didn't yell, and I was not even angry, but I couldn't tolerate any more disrespect. I needed to show a firm stance, and I wasn't in the mood to compromise.

"I know alot of things has happened in my absence, and I fully intend to take care of the situation. I hold this meeting to inform you I will begin my campaign to make education accessible for women all over Ghana, not just Kumasi, as I promised. We also need to show our solidarity with the Liberian people. So I intend to invite President George Weah to the palace. We need to control the situation and smooth things over. Any objections?"

I had it in my mind that I would face opposition from the moment I entered, but I was in no mood for the foolery. This was happening, and I was going to make sure that everything went as I planned. None of them even spoke up. My demeanor must have made them realize that I·was serious and wouldn't be entertaining their usual questioning attitude. "Good," I said and walked off.

I had already taken care of the invite to President Weah. Now it was time to campaign. First, I had to address my people. My mother helped me made all the arrangements and instructed some local media to be present. I got on the phone with the Liberian president, not knowing what to expect. I wasn't sure if Femi's lies had gotten to him or not, but I was determined to remain civilized and be supportive. I planned to be honest with him and tell him the truth, but a part of me hesitated. The last thing I wanted was for Liberia to take advantage of the domestic turmoil I had in the palace. I couldn't imagine him wanting to leave his country during these times of tragedy, but I had to try.

This was important. I explained the importance of the meeting to him, and thankfully, he was more than understanding of the situation. All I had to do was wait.

Given the situation, it didn't surprise me to find out t an elder had requested to see me. "What can I do for you, Elder Kofi?" I said when he entered the room.

"My queen, I want to tell you, you have my full support even though there are a lot of things I wish were different," he said timidly.

"Like my brother being king instead of me, right?" I questioned with annoyance. I fully intended to hear the truth come out of his mouth.

He sighed. "That is one thing I would not change. You were chosen for this. It is time you understood and accepted that this didn't happen at chance. I cannot keep it to myself any longer."

Feeling more confused than before, I looked at him. "What are you talking about?" he sighed heavily and began.

"Many years ago, there was a prophecy from the high priest that a woman would become queen and lead the country because the men who were placed in charge of the throne allowed the British to enslave our men, rape our women, and abuse our children. The gods of our land had had enough of it. They said that if the men couldn't save and protect this country, a woman would.

"When the high priest told us this, the entire community fell into turmoil. Half of the elders didn't care because deep down, they thought it would never happen. The prophecy shook the others as they spread the news. The prophecy was so disruptive it drove people to protest.

"Eventually, the tribal groups began acting by secretly killing women and children at nighttime. Even though the entire town knew about it, nothing was said or done about it. One day, the tribal groups became bold. They started killing publicly by going into homes and attacking women. Specifically, the first born daugher of every tribe. The chaos lasted for seven days, and by the end, they had killed over three thousand women and female children. The town mourned for years. And because of these atrocities, the gods punished our land with poverty and famine. It wasn't until your father became king that things looked favorable to us." I felt my legs going numb. "Why is that? What did he do?"

"Your father remained in the shrine and fasted for thirty-nine days. Sacrificing three virgin men he attoned for our sins after. No king before your father was ever willing to do this, but he chose to. The gods valued his gesture but denied his request. Women had suffered unimaginable pain in our land. So they demanded all firstborn sons of each tribe be sacrificed as an atonement since the tribe responsible could not be solely identified. Unfortunately, this included your father's tribe."

"Wait. What?" I asked, shocked.

He nodded. "Hmm. For weeks, your father fought and argued until finally, he convinced the tribe to do this, and they did."

"So how is Femi still alive?"

"That will have to be a conversation between you and the high priest."

"Elder Kofi, you need to tell me. How is Femi still alive?"

"Your father agreed with the gods."

"What type of agreement?" I demanded.

"To allow your brother to live. Your father agreed to give you the royal birth mark instead of Femi."

"What?" I yelled.

"He kept Femi alive. Even if he wasn't going to be king. He believed that if a woman was going to bring change and fullfil the prophecy, it would be you."

The First Act

Elder Kofi left and I stood there engrossed. He dropped a bombshell on me and left me to deal with the truth. I had no idea this was the reason they had chosen me as queen. He had given me a definitive way to eliminate Femi; perhaps he would understand if I told him the truth. He would know what our Father did was to keep his sorry ass alive.

Even still, I could never tell him. If my father wanted him to know, he would've told him. Regardless of how much I wanted to hurt him the way he did me, I just couldn't. This was not the way, but I wondered *Where the hell my mother fit in all of this?*

Having committed these sins against the gods of our land was an enormous thing. I knew once my Dad made that agreement, he would honor it . They had already cursed this land once, and I was the ultimate sacrifice to appease them. They were adamant the firstborn men from all the tribes were to be sacrificed to make up for the atrocities committed, and the burden of the throne fell on me. I felt it was unjust on their part. Did no one else wonder if I may have wanted a different life? They had chosen me as a queen as punishment to our men. No wonder they hated me. I was a reminder of the prophecy made years ago. The one that killed hundreds of women to ensure it never came to pass and casued our men to be sacrificed. In some odd ways, it assured me of my right to the throne, if not more, than Femi. Regardless, the gods had chosen me, and I knew they'd be with me through the inevitable backlash I was bound to face.

I pushed these thoughts aside; my self-pity days were over. I needed to focus. I had the meeting with the Liberian president coming up, and that was the only thing I needed to worry about o now. My lack of a good judge of character caused all those people to lose their lives. Even though I had done everything from my end to ensure thilives could be safe. I'd chosen Femi, and I'd failed.

With that in mind, I closed my eyes and hoped sleep would carry me away. "Tomorrow would be a hectic day," I said to myself as I thought of organizing campaigns all over the city to remind my people I hadn't forgotten about the promise I made to them. I wondered if Femi would do anything to disrupt those campaigns. I would need to have extra security in place to ensure it didn't happen.

*****

The next day went by in a blur. Moments after I had woken up, I stood in front of a massive crowd. I had to address the obvious before I could hope to get them interested in anything else I had to say. How was I supposed to tell them everything? Saying anything could put my entire country in jeopardy, so I had no choice but to address it briefly.

"I would like to thank all of you for coming. I've been absent since my coronation. However, I assure you this was in favor of us all. My goal is to begin fullfilling the promise I made to you: to make education for women accessible throughout our community."

At this, the women in the crowd cheered, and the men were in opposition hung their heads in disapproval. "I would like all of you to look at the bigger picture. If you think the men who go to war are the ones on whose back this country is built, then you may be right. In courage, the men of this country are unparalleled. They have defended this country many times and are some of the strongest men in the world.

"Their courage, tenacity, and strength are admirable. But now, I must ask more from you. For a country to progress, workforce and technological intelligence must go hand in hand. We cannot go forward without thinking about the future. If we proceed blindly, we risk economic stagnant. If not now, then surely.

"We have good lands. We have good hard-working people, and we have resources. We can make our country the best in the world. If our women do not have access to basic right to education, we have failed. We need to make sure that the women and children have the rights and the means to take us forward. We must step out of the comfort of old means, and we must move toward new traditions.

"To do this, we must make education accessible to everyone. We must make sure they have the tools to teach and help the children so we can become doctors, engineers, lawyers, diplomats, scientists, and be at the foremost in every field."

I had already memorized an entire speech by heart. Yet as I stood before my people, I spoke from my heart. I needed to make sure that everyone understood I wanted nothing more for this country than the absolute best. I would have to work to ensure that it happened. The time was long gone when Ghana used to be considered a country of the poor. I knew the image the world conjured in their minds when they thought about Africa as a whole, but change was coming, and it would start with the Ashanti Region.

As I looked over the crowd, I could tell my message had touched hearts. They were all cheering, and I wondered if this was the moment that my father lived for. Maybe these moments kept us going when we saw the sheer joy and jubilation ofur people. This is what gave us the power to keep going. Their joy was our strenght.

After my speech, the elders who had accompanied me spoke a few words of their own, confirming support of everything I said and assured the people that this was the way to move forward in becoming the rugged region we once were. Their sponsorship and approval were refreshing, and I was glad for it.

*****

I sat up in bed, having awoken from a nightmare. I hadn't realized just how late I slept in. When I glanced at the clock, I only had a few hours to get ready until I met with the president. I made our meeting private. I needed to take care of this situation once and for all. Coupled with the my women's rights initiative's, such a diplomatic success would give me leverage to bargain with the elders to allow me to continue leading a double lifestyle until my contract with the navy was over. All I needed was about two more years of this constant back-and-forth travel, and I could stay in my birth country and rule my people.

The Liberian president entered the room and walked toward me. I had never met him before, but I heard from the elders he was a good man. My guard was up as my father had taught me. Trust no man. My only prayer was that Femi hadn't gotten to him before I could. "Mr. President, it is good to meet you," I said, smiling warmly and shaking his hand.

"Likewise. I would have thought this would have been a public meeting," he said with his eyebrows creeping up his forehead.

"You wouldn't want to be harassed by the media now, would you?" I asked, smiling a little.

He laughed as well and said, affably, "No, I have had it about up to here with the media for now."

"Good," I said. "Mr. President, my advisors." I introduced him to all the elders in the room including Kofi. "I would like to extend my deep condolences for the recent attacks by the Americans. I want you to know we will extend our aid to you and your people. We are sister countries, and we must support one another, especially in times like this."

Though I had all the time in the world, I wanted this over with quickly. I needed the elders to hear what I had to say and be done with this meeting.

"Thank you, Your Majesty. I can't express how much the gestures mean to Liberia," he said.

I felt a sense of gentilness in him for his people. "Perhaps you're right. I didn't," I said, raising my voice a little so that everyone in the room could hear. They had no idea what I had in mind; I wanted to give them a surprise before bringing up the matter of my living arrangement. "I am sure the recent change of rule with the Ashanti people took aback you."

"Yes. At first, we all thought it was a joke," he said confidently. "Well, as you can see, it's not." "You're familiar with Femi, my brother. You, along with everyone expected him to take the throne. He did not! Anyways, the recent attack on Liberia has put me in a bit of a moral dilemma. I had no intention of allowing this to happen."

With every word I spoke, the president appeared to become more and more confused.

"I am part of the US military—to be specific, the navy—and I have some important information regarding some of their operations that could prove beneficial to you. I recognized how much pain they have caused your country, and I want to make amends. This is my way of extending my hand of friendship for all our future endeavors," I clarified. There was no need for elaboration. He was a smart man, and he knew how vital this proposition was.

I wanted so badly to expose the cowardly and weak-minded brother of mine, but I realized that everyone's mistakes were mine to shoulder as a leader. To tell him it was Femi's choice to allow them to die would make me look bad. I would be signing his death warrant. Femi was my demon to deal with. He was my brother, and not even his betrayal could erase the love I had for him. "Please, believe me, I would not have invited you here if my intentions were ill-willed."

"I see. What intelligence do you have about the Americans?" he asked, and I immediately knew this meeting was a success.

I disclosed a few details about US operations conducted in Liberia. My actions surprised even the elders. I hoped that my actions showed them I was committed to Ghana and to Africa most of all. I got that meeting over with over as quickly as I could. I needed to talk with the elders alone. So, I sent word for the rest of the elders to gather in the throne room.

"This meeting was for your benefit. I am the queen of this land. My people and their interest will always come first. Considering recent events, understand that I will be going back to the States. Not now, but soon. I will return from time to time, and I want you to know how important this is. I need to there because we need access to thier intel. This is my decision as to your queen. Are we clear?"

Not a single one of them spoke up; instead, they all got up and knelt before me as a gesture of respect.

*****

For the next two years, I went back and forth between Ghana and the United States. I still had about a year and some months left on my naval contract. In that time, I had won most of the people over, yet some of them believed that I was too Americanized.

My brother was still up to his no-good, mischievous ways. He had gotten my uncle on his side, and together, they were going mad about my being unfit to rule. During my coronation, I had made sure that everyone from my family had pledged their allegiance to me, yet he had convinced my uncle to break that sacred oath.

On my routine trip to Ghana, they informed me about a protest near the palace led by my brother and uncle. He had even gotten some elders on his side advising him. The diplomatic success meant nothing to them. They claimed that an Ashanti ruler should not leave their post so often. He even spoke against my decision to invite my friends here from time to time. I was a nontraditional leader who needed to be dealt with byany means neccessary.

I had enough of Femi and his immaturity. The initiative I took for the women's education rights was going well. Everything I promised I would do, I was doing. What more did he want? All he wanted to be was the king, regardless of the cost. He was not the same brother I once knew. Ignoring is insolence was costing me.

As I stood in the doorway of my palace filled with anger watching my brother, I called out to the general. "Arrest them all! Now!" Femi was facing the crowd, urging them on to cotinue screaming and protest. Within moments, the general had mobilized the troops to form ranks and move toward them. Seeing the men in uniform with guns and weapons some of them became afraid.

I shouted to the general, "Round them all up!" I had to show a force of power; I was over and done with this nonsense. All I felt was an uncontrolled rage. I wanted to show to my uncle, my brother, and everyone els continued to opposed me I was not to be taken lightly. I was the queen—their queen!—chosen by the gods.

The soldiers threw tear gas into the crowd, and I saw my uncle running back. Femi, ever stubborn, was urging them all to stay put. He had seen war, but most of these people hadn't. Seeing the oncoming soldiers, they lost their nerve and fled. The soldiers could only round up some elders, along with Femi.

I was looking at them, and I immediately gave the order. "Throw them all in jail and put Femi in the palace cell." I turned and returned to my chambers. Pacing back and forth, I felt sick to my stomach thinking of the force and method I had to resort to. Seeing my people run in fear from men under my orders made me want to vomit. But, God, I was sick of it! Yet I allowed my mother's words to guilt me into allowing Femi to stay at the palace cell instead of the public jail. I thought, *If he wants to act like a fool, treat him like one.*

I heard a knock and immediately responded, "Enter."

"Asha, you cannot do this!" my mother shouted and barged in.

"Mom, please don't start." Her tone only aggrevated me more. To do anything other than stand by my choices would prove me weak. That was the last thing I needed.

"Yaa Asantewaa, I am your mother! Even if you're queen, I am still your mother, and I am telling you, do not do this." she pleaded.

I could see the tears in her eyes. No matter what Femi did, she would always love him. But Femi wasn't my son! He was hers. He may still be my brother, but for now, he was a traitor, and I doubt even the gods would allow me to pardon him. I had already been generous enough by allowing him to live this far. Tradition demanded his death. How could I kill my brother under the same traditional laws that said a woman was worthless? The same rules I was trying to change.

My head ached, thinking of all this. "Mum, you know I can't go back on what I did. I did nothing when he betrayed me, but now he is actively opposing me. I can't tolerate it. This is all we will discuss on the matter." I said with finality.

"What if he apologizes publicly?" she asked.

"We'll see. I'm sorry it's come to this." That was all I could say. I couldn't undo anything or ignore his behav-or, but I still was sorry.

Weeping loudly, she walked away and left. Within a moment, she was back with Femi and the general with her. That was it.

"How dare you let this prisoner come out of his cell!" I roared. I did not even want to see his face.

My mother shouted, "You need to hear him out."

I expected the entire palace could hear us by now. There was always a gray line between being a national ruler and having to still listen to your mother. I knew her well. Though she respected my position, she often took advantage of her role as a mother in my life. She was the only person who could yell at me and demand anything. Seeing Femi in front of me, bound and on his knees, I felt conflicted. "Leave us," I said to the guard.

"Femi, please speak," my mother said still teary-eyed.

"It was my birthright. You stole it," he said, his voice quivering. This was the same conversation we had after my coronation, and I thought he and I were okay. Here we are again!

Feeling irritated, I snapped. "So that justified you to let all those Liberians die? Stab me in the back? Oppose me? Go back on your oath? You have no honor. Femi."

"What exactly did you expect? I no longer consider you my sister, just as you no longer consider me your brother. You stole my birthright," he said heatedly.

I wanted so much to slap the life out of him and have him thrown in the forest for his stupidity. "I stole? I stole your birthright? They gave it to me! Not even our father could have changed that. Get over it, and get over yourself," I spat out mercilessly.

"Asha, please control yourself," I heard mother began to speak.

"No! He betrayed me and opposed me. He's still acting like a child. He can't even bring himself to admit that he's wrong. I will not have that."

My words hurt him. He hung his head low. When he looked up at me, I noticed his eyes were rimmed red. "You could have given me the throne. You didn't have to take the damn throne!"

"You know what! Shut up! Just shut up! You want to know the truth? Why the gods chose me and not you?

"Asha, do not speak of anything you cannot take back. Do not undo history with your temper."

I could feel my mother's voice filled with caution, pain, and anger, but I didn't care.

"You wanna know the truth? Ask Mom. She should know."

"Ask me what? I know nothing about anything."

Femi glanced at my mother, she looked away, and they both turned to look in my direction.

"Fine, I'll tell you," I said, and in a blind rage, I told him every-thing Elder Kofi told me regarding the prophecy.

The Heartbreak

Femi looked at me with disgust, shame, confusion, and regret. I had just told him why I was chosen to lead our people instead of him. In all honesty, had the sitution been reversed, I might have lost my damn mind. I could see the despair in his eyes. My memores of this onc swwet boy who had always protected me and made me laugh was overshadowed by the pain our father caued him.

I, along with my father and the gods had ruined Femi. My brother's heart was broken, yet I felt no regret. What was done was done.

My mother was looking at Femi. I wondered what she knew about this and why she's kept quiet all this time. Part of me hoped didn't know. I could never forgive her.

Femi seemed to have lost his ability to speak. "There, now you know. They did all this to save your sorry ass. Now get out of my sight."

My anger had overtaken me, and not even my mom could convince me to make amends with him. If there were any chance of reconciliation, it would have to be from him.

"Asha!" my mother said, shocked.

"What! You expect me to have sympathy? or feel bad? I didn't say this to hurt him. Regardless of what you may think, I said it because he needs to understand it was never about his pride. It has always been about him. His life."

I was too angry, much too frustrated, and too exhausted to keep it in any longer. I had spent my entire life being the puppet to others' wishes, and now it was my family who were causing me headaches.

"Why did you not tell me this before?" Femi asked, with his eyes still fixed to the floor.

"Why? So you'd have another reason to wallow in self-pity? I already told you, Femi. I had no interest in becoming queen. I was here because dad was dying, and I wanted to see him before it s too late. I didn't come here for any of this. You couldn't understand that then, and you still can't understand. You can't see beyond your interest. If this is who you are now, then Dad made the right call. I am glad he chose me to lead."

Built-up resentment gushed out. I tried to make him feel the hurt I had been feeling. Th constant betrayal from him and the sleepless nights.

"I am sorry," Femi said. I was about to interrupt him when he made a gesture tocontinue speaking. "I agree with you. I have made many choices since the day you were crowned. I let anger consume me and I allowed that to drive me. I cannot apologize enough, but I understand that I must be punished for what I've done."

He stopped talking, and ou eyes met. The time was long gone when I would trust people just based on my relationship with them. If my brother could betray me, I couldn't easily trust anyone else. People change with circumstances. Those who would once give their lives to save you, could also conspire to end you. I learned to trust with gut, the one thing I could rely on and the one thing that had never betrayed me. But as I looked into Femi's eyes, it all settled.

Before, he thought he still had a right to the throne; hat was logical to him. He was fighting for his bithright. I was the one who had stolen that right. Now that he knew that he had no right to the throne, was he content? I wondered how hard it would have been for him to go against his own family, fighting for what he believed to be right. I still couldn't justify his actions, but it made sense. He was content following me, standing behind me, and supporting me in leading the country that we both loved dearly. He wanted what h assumed was his.

Once more, Femi spoke. "I went back on my word. I pledged allegiance to you, and I broke it. I led protests against you, and I knowingly misled you. That is treason. I believe we both know the punishment for that sister." he said.

I knew what he wasimplying. If he were given the ultimate punishment for treason, he would have paid foris sins in this world. That would wipe the slate clean. He would be in bliss in the afterlife. That was our faith.

"Atoning for your sins after you've committed them? Tell me, what do I get out of that?" I asked. I figured he would be of great use to me, although with Femi, nothing was ever for sure. Against my better judgment, I found forgiveness and leniency creeping into my heart.

"You should send a message that all those who oppose you will meet their rightful end. Also, I am going to make a public statement in your favor that I have chosen this for myself, that I was the wrong one, and I now have to pay the price," he said.

"So all the years spent training you, teaching you our traditions and customs, all the resources spent by this family in making you into a man of substance—I'm just supposed to let all of that go to waste by killing you?"

"You don't have any other choice," he said.

"General!" I shouted. The door immediately opened, and the general came in. He had already unclasped his gun and was holding it in his hand, fully prepared for any situation that could have presented itself. "Calm down," I said.

When he came in, he pointed his gun directly toward Femi. My mother, seeing this, immediately covered Femi with her body and stood protectively over him.

"Mother get away from him. This has nothing to do with you." When she didn't move, I yelled, "Move away!"

She was still looking at me tearfully. She couldn't even say anything and slowly moved away, her eyes silently begging me not to harm him.

"Cut his restraints," I ordered the general, who then looked at me with disapproval.

I understood his hesitation. It was out of care for me. He was the general of our armies since my father's time and was one of his closest friends. I was practically like a daughter to him. Hell, even I was rethinking my decision. Was this something I could live with for the rest of my life? He timidly moved forward and cut his restraints.

Femi stood still; he was prepared for his end. He was looking at me rey to accept his fate. He was ready to die. In our tribe, deaths for sins committed were attonments enough. That was the norm, and even though I had let go of most tradition. Femi would settle his debt, and he would do it for the rest of his life. Just not the way he thought.

"Get up and kneel before me," I said, my voice reverberating loudly in the room.

He got up and strolled toward me. The general followed closely behind him. I believed in redmption. He knelt before me. "Pledge allegiance to me," I said and had the strangest sense of déjà vu as if it was my coronation all over again.

He knelt before, pledging his allegiance to me. "Everyone in this room will bear witness to your pledge. You are going to serve under me for the rest of your life, and you are going to do so with honor, observing the traditions taught to us by our father and mother. The morals with which we live our lives and the morals with which we give our life."

He looked up at me. shining as if being reborn.

"Nation before self!" I shouted.

"Nation before self!" I felt strengthened by the voices of my brother, my mother, the general, and all the soldiers outside who heard me and reeated after me.

In that moment, I beieved to have gained my brother back. I was relieved. It would still be facing lot of problems but at least for now, I had my family's support—fully. The complete and unwavering support I always wanted. That was what mattered the most.

Femi got up and hugged me, and I hugged him back as tightly as I could. In my heart, I could feel my decision was right. "I suppose we should notify the elders of this. We have our family back again."

"Before we do that, Asha, I need to talk to you," my mother said. "Privately, if Your Majesty will allow." She looked at Femi and the general.

"Of course, Queen Mother," the general said. "You can have my old room, Femi. It was always better than yours" I said, lightly jabbing at him.

"Thank you, Your Highness." he said. Even though things were sorte out between us, it would take a long time for things to go back to how they used to be. *Well, better late than never*, I thought.

After they all left the room, my mother ran toward me and hugged me, ultimately breaking down and saying something which I did not understand one bit. "Mum, it's okay. He's my brother. I could never order his death. Did you think I would?" I asked.

She was still crying, and I gently guided her toward a seat and helped her sit down. I wanted to tell her something that would give her peace, but I could understand how she felt. "Serwaa!" I called, and one of my maids came in with a glass of water, knelt beside my mother, and gently put it on her lips.

Sh took the glass in her hand. "Asha, I love you. I can't thank you enough. Your father would be proud of you. You did the right thing"

This was the best compliment a queen could get. "I love you too, Mother," I replied. "You could have said that in front of Femi, you know.y ou didnt have to snd hem awaay" I wanted to get the conversation going so she would stop crying.

"That's not what I wanted to talk to you about" I could sense the change of mood in the room. She was nervous.

"What is it?" I urged feing nervous myself.

"It's about Jay," she said, regaining her composure. "You aren't just friends. I know that."

"Mum, I'm not havintisconversation with you."

"You know,as Queen you, will have to marry a man from here, one of our own. You cannot marry an American," she said, looking at me.

Wow, I thought. *Not a minute had gone by since dealing with this Femi problem, and I am plunged into another one.* It was as if God was just thinking up ways to make my life more difficult. I had no idea what I was supposed to say now, and I sure as hell wasn' going to say anythng that would ensure my mother I ageedwith her demands. Jay and I had been through too much. Thwas out he question.

"Mum, This conversation is over. I've been through alot, and he's been by my side for all of it. What you're asking is not possible." I said. *God!* My entire life was under scrutiny. *Why the hell do people always have to tell me what to do? Always!*

Sadly, no matter how much I argued with them, this was not something they would compromise on. And with everything I was dealing with, I haven't had the chance to even think about it. "I can't hear this," I said with pain and frustration in my eyes.

"All right. But know, this isn't over. You are queen, my dear. Consider the nation before yourself." she said and left.

I resented her for saying this. How could I let go of Jay after eveything? He committed treason and risked his entire career, so I could try to save the Liberians from a terrible fate. He was the same person who had protected me after learning of my true identity, not to mention the friendship, love, and connection we shared. *Do they expect me to give him up just like that for a stranger because of my traditions? Hell no!*

I pushed these thoughts from my mind. It had been a long day, and I needed to sleep. Maybe my mother would come to her senses by tomorrow.

*****

If someone had told me being queen came with restless sleep, I probably would have given up the throne to just about anyone. Even in my sleep, nightmares plagued me. I was being separated from Jay and thrust into the arms of a man. I tried to look at his face, but I couldn't picture it. All I knew was that I didn't want to be away from Jay. I felt like a little girl who was being taken from her secure surroundings, given up by her loved ones. History was repeating itself.

My eyes opened for what felt like a second after they had closed. I heard a knock on my door. I got up groggily. I thought sleep was supposed to refresh you, not give you a damn headache. "Enter!"

A maid entered, and behind her was my mother. "Okay, so you aren't even going to let me refresh before getting back on my case."

"Asha, you need to come with me," she said hurriedly. Something was wrong.

"What happened?"

"You need to speak with the elders. They are assembled in the throne room. They want to talk about the 'Jay' situation." she said, looking directly at me.

I knew that this was not her doing, but I didn't care. "Mum! You woke me up for this?" I had it up to here with these silly meetings. I didn't get the prejudice against me being with someone who was not from Ghana; it was honestly absurd.

"I didn't call them here. They just came. You know how important these things are. They are demanding your presence," she said, coming forward and holding my hand.

"Fine, I will talk to them." "Please go ask the elders to await my presence. The queen who isn't allowed to sleep needs to use the bathroom." I said glowering. "Give me two minutes. I need to make myself presentable." I slowly took my time in refreshing myself and got dressed, then started for the throne room.

I stopped and thought about what I wanted. I wanted to stay with Jelani, and they would have to deal with it. *Nation before self!* The words reverberated in my mind. I was their leader. To go against our belief would have a price I couldn't pay.

It wasn't as if being with Jay would affect the way I ruled this country. Much the opposite, it might make me a better leader. They need to understand that he is an essential part of me.

Queens don't cry. They prevail. My father's advice to me had been haunting me. I now understood why those words meant so much to me and why my father had said them. He knew there would be many moments that would cause me to want to give up. The burden of an entire country was on my shoulders, and no matter how much I kidded myself, I would still be alone in bearing this burden. It was mine, and honestly, that was as much a source of pride as it was a burden.

I walked toward the throne room, where all the elders were assembled. "I was told that my presence was requested," I said as soon as I sat on my throne. I looked around and saw my family already seated with the elders. I much rather they were by my side but I already knew where they stood on this matter.

"My queen." Elder Kofi stood up. "We need to discuss a crucial matter with you."

I remained quiet. They would be the ones who were going to bring this up. I would rather be anywhere in the world than here.

"We need to discuss your marriage. A ruler cannot lead without a partner. We have chosen the best man for you we wish you to marry. The people have talked about your life and your friends from America. They have been seen coming in and out of the palace, which does not exactly inspire confidence in us. There's a rumor that you have intentions to bring a stranger into our palace. This cannot happen," he said.

I could tell he was uncomfortable. However, being the most senior in the room, the responsibility fell on his shoulders. "There has been talk among the people regarding your colleague from America, the one called Jelani. I think it's now time to squash these rumors, and the best way to do that would be for you to get married to a man from here."

He was about to continue when another elder stood up and interrupted him. "My queen, it is vital for the growth of our country. There have been many things in your reign that have gone against our traditions, and we cannot allow this to be one of them. We need to finish this matter once and for all."

I looked at my mother and immediately knew that this was the elder who had come to the palace complaining.

"Is there anything else that you would like to say?" I asked with no expression. If I were to take control of this situation, I would probably make it worse. I thought, *Let's just hear what they have to say.*

"Yes, my queen. We know how hard it is for you, but as you know, the nation comes before our interest. That is the burden we must face for being given a power position that we cannot escape. If you can understand that, would you like us to introduce you to the man we think is the best person for you to help assist you in leading our country?"

"Not to say you can't do it alone." Another elder quickly added.

Before I even knew what I was saying, I replied, "Please bring him in."

The elder signaled for the guard to bring him in and they returned with a face I had not seen since my childhood. It was Akwasi. I immediately recognized him because he was the son of the general.

Femi and I used to play with him when we were younger, and he would have been considered my best friend, second to my brother. However, after I had gone to the States, I had completely lost contact with about everyone and had barely given any thought to anyone back from Ghana. Akwasi was probably the last one on my mind.

"Akwasi, it is nice to see you again," I said looking at him. I knew that it would didn't want to insult him by not acknowledging him. I couldn't do that to the general, who was looking at his son with great pride and a smile on his face.

"Likewise, my queen," he said in a deep, rumbling voice. He was man every woman dreamed of being with. He had a deep, slow rumbling voice coupled with his massive figure and perfect body, which made him the most intimidating man in the room. I looked at him and my brother and remembered how they used to play fight, which would almost always be broken up because both of them refused to give up. My brother wasn't small by any standard, but Akwasi was even bigger than him, and I wondered who would win if they were to fight now.

"Is that all?" I said looking about in the room, refusing to meet the general's eyes. I respected and loved him. However, marriage was about more than appreciation and respect. This was going to ruin my entire life. I would have to do everything I could to stop it.

"Yes, my queen." Elder Kofi said at once, earning hard looks from the rest of the elders.

"Thank you. You are all dismissed." I get up and discreetly gesturing my mother to follow me. I went back to my room and awaited my mother, who followed shortly.

"You are not seriously going to make me go through with this right?" I said in disbelief.

"I am! You must!" she demanded.

"Asha, you are queen. There are some things that even you cannot escape."

Before I could convince the elders, I would have to convince my mother. "Look, you have no idea how much Jelani has done for me and this country. He put his life on the line for this country to save people he's never met. That's the man he is. He's always protected me. And I love him. I'm in love with him, which, apparently, as the queen, doesn't even matter to anyone. But I thought it would matter to you." I looked at her with disappointment.

"If this were Femi, he would be free to choose whoever he wanted." I cried. "Why do I have to be treated differently, like I don't matter? Femi would never be subjected to this kind of treatment." I stopped, seeing my mother's hands were raised.

"Look, dear. Yes, things may have been different had Femi ruled. But the reality is you are the ruler, not Femi. As far as Jelani goes, no matter how much he did, He is still not of you people. You may have asked him to, but it was for saving the life of innocents. If he had any shred of humanity, he would've done th samefor anyone else."

"But that's precisely what he did. I didn't even have—"

"And there you have it. Look, I have nothing against Jelani, but you are the queen of this nation," she said, emphasizing the word nation. "Realize that. You must understand, I take no pleasure in this happening to you. I know how much you have been through, and I do not want to put you through anything more, but not even your father, God bless his soul, would've been able to help you escape this."

I looked at my mother, knowing that I had lost the battle. I would have to let go of Jelani, and the thought made me want to die.

The Mission

I wanted it all to end—the pain, the suffering, the problems that arose one after the other, and the never-ending expectations that seemed forced down my throat. What was it to the elders, to my mother, to the entire country whom I wanted to be with? It was my personal life, and I had the right to live it the way I wanted.

I couldn't seem to wrap my head around the fact that I would no longer be with Jelani. I had no idea how I was going to have this painful conversation with him. How the hell was I supposed to break his heart? It would crush him to know this wasn't even my decision.

If I refused, it would leave my countrymen unsure of me, and I knew one thing for sure: the needs of many took precedence over the needs of the few. I was the few, or rather, the one whose needs were to be put last. My marriage to one of my own would cement my position as my people's leader, and it would confirm to the elders I held my country's interest above my own. It felt as if every aspect of my life was being dictated. They would not rest until they had completely molded me into a complete Ghanaian they saw fit to rule. This is exactly why I hadn't returned for ages. Back in the States, you were as free as the decisions you made.

I had to talk to Jelani to explain the entire situation. For the first time in my life, I was at a complete mess. I had no idea how I would start. "Hey, Jay, I know you have done a lot for me, but unfortunately, my elders are demanding I leave you to marry another. Sorry. Have a good life.

This situation tore me up inside. I felt terrible that Jay was even here with me. I didn't even have the luxury of telling my mother that it would have to wait until I saw him again. He was literally in the palace, with no idea what was happening or what was being discussed about him.

I made my way toward his room to talk to him. I told him everything. He stood there looking at me. "So wait, you're breaking up with me because a bunch of old men asked you to?" he asked.

He was clear on what I had said, but I knew he still wouldn't understand. That was one thing about African culture. Everyone wanted to be a part of it, but they weren't ready to accept everything that came with being an African. Regardless of what I wanted to do, seeing the pain in his eyes, I couldn't answer him the way tradition demanded me to.

"No, what I'm saying is I need time. We need a plan," I said. I thought I would feel as regretful as I had when I talked to my mom, but being the queen had even stripped me of that. I had to hide my emotions; embracing them would make this even harder than I wanted it to be. I had to push someone I loved away to protect my throne.

"You know what, Asha, It's completely fine. I've been thinking about this since the day of your coronation. I had an idea something like this would happen, but I always thought our bond was stronger than that. Never did I imagine you would agree so freely to marry someone else because of traditions. I guess that's how things work with your people. I can't pretend to understand your situation. I never had the burden of an entire country on my shoulders, but I suppose you have bigger things to worry about than a simple relationship you've dedicated years to. That's fine with me. I just need to know that you'll be able to do right by your country, no matter what, and may you never lose your inheritance because of love."

His words cut me deeply, I could have died. He understood yet couldn't hide his disappointment in me. At that very moment, I wished I weren't of royal birth. I had allowed my traditions to betray the one person who loved me even before they knew who I was. If the roles were reversed, I don't know if I could handle it. My traditions had severed our ties, and it made me sick to have allowed it.

"I will leave as soon as I have made arrangements," he added. I could imagine how hard it would be for him to stay here. I considered offering to drop him off at the airport, but I understood his nature; he wouldn't have liked to accept my help. So I nodded, and he turned around, gathering his things.

On impulse, I ran and hugged him. I didn't know if that was the best decision, but I didn't care. He kissed me forhead and hugged me. Given a choice, I could have stayed there with him for an entire lifetime. In that one kiss, we told each other everything that could never be put into words. It was probably the most excruciating moment of my life. I wanted to cry, not out of mere sadness but the feeling that my heart had been ripped into pieces. I tried to destroy everything in sight and condemn everyone involved to an early grave. I had never been so sad and furious at the same time. *Queens don't cry. They prevail.* I backed off gently and looked at him. "I love you."

"I love you too. I hope one day, you're strong enough to overrule your traditions. Don't let it change who you are." he replied, and without even bothering to pick up his things left the room.

*****

I went back into my room and got in my bed. Staring up at the ceiling, I tried my best not to cry. Everything was frozen. I wanted to sleep so I could at least forgo this feeling of numbness, but even sleep seemed to have deserted me, so I just lay there. I could feel the light of the sun going out. If there were any other important matters to attend to, I didn't hear about them. I wanted nothing more than to burst into tears. I was utterly alone, reliving my tragic roy mancestor repeatedly.

It took me a moment to realize that something was disturbing me. I sat up and realized that my phone was ringing. I had no inten-tion of answering it until I saw it was Commander Breeden. "Yes?" I said after picking up. Speaking to a superior officer, the formal greeting would have been more respectful, but I didn't care. My heart was broken. *To hell with everyone.*

"Asha, I need you to report immediately," he said.
"Is everything okay?" I asked. The last time this had happened, there had been an intel attack. *What it was this time?*

"It's good news! So get here ASAP," he said, and the line went dead.

What could be of such good news to require my prompt presence? I thought as I got out of my bed. This could not have come at a better time. I hated lying in bed, wallowing in self-pity. I'd have to talk to my mother about this and tell her I would be leaving again. I made my way toward the door, but then I thought better of it and told the maid to summon my family so I could talk to them.

Shortly after getting changed and ready to leave, I heard a knock on the door and told them to enter. "Jelani is gone. I hope you're happy," I said, glaring at my mom. "Anyway, I have to go back to the States. You guys are in charge." I saw that my mother was about to say something, but I held my hand up. "I will hear nothing more from you. I wouldn't be leaving if I didn't have to. I asked Jay to leave, and that is done. I'll get back as soon as I can, then we will see about this marriage. If the elders have a problem with it, tell them to do something about it." I walked toward the door. Just as I was about to open it, I felt a hand on my shoulder and saw that it was Femi. "What?"

"Asha, I can understand what you have been through. I'm sorry. Be back soon." my mother said.

It wasn't her fault, but there was too much pain regarding the situation, I couldn't handle talking about it any longer.

I go on the plane and headed for the States. I wondered what it would be like to face Jay again after what happened. Could we even be friends? I pushed these thoughts out of my mind and sat in my seat waiting. We landing in DC sortly after.

I walked into Breeden's office and saw Maya was already there. Breeden seemed excited to see me. Maya was nervous and trying to hide it. "Asha, good! You're here," Breeden said.

"What was so urgent, sir?" I said after saluting.

"Maya, will you do the honors?" Breeden said, smiling.

"Well, I have great news."

"We've found several historical artifacts that we need to retrieve," she said, walking over to Breeden's desk and picking up a file. She handed it to me.

There were several pictures in the file, and they looked like African artifacts. My father had been after some of these artifacts for a long time. It was another reason he hadn't oppose to me joining the military; he'd urged me to trace where they were. I looked at all the pictures, identifying which ones belonged to my people, to my palace. Some of them looked familiar. I looked up and understood why Maya looked the way she did.

"We are putting together a team so we can get them back. " Breeden continued.

"They are going back to the museums they were taken from. We need to put together a team and get them back asap!" Maya added.

"How did you guys find this?" I asked. I had done practically everything in my power to locate these, and I'd still been unsuccessful.

114

"We've been looking for a long time, but with no luck. Just two days ago, I received intel from a CI."

"Who?" I asked.

"About ten years ago, I was on the field for a classified operation and made friends with an FBI agent. He was the one who gave me this intel. It is a reliable source, and we need to track this down immediately." he replied.

"Then what's the holdup?" I said.

"We already have a plan. Maya's in charge of the team. She'll brief you on it. The rest is up to you." he concluded and we both saluted him before exiting his office.

I thought we were going to the briefing room, but Maya led me straight out of the building. I assumed she wanted to talk about the artifacts. "What's the plan?" I said, pretending I didn't know what this was all about.

"We have the location of these artifacts. It's in Afghanistan, in the hands of the Taliban. But I can fill you in later. Don't pretend you don't know why I brought you here."

"What, Maya?"

"Look, I respect you, and I respect your position in Ghana, but my loyalties still lie with the United States. I'm going to make one thing clear: I need to know that you will do nothing to sabotage this operation."

"You say that they stole these artifacts from a museum in the United States. So basically, you're launching a mission to retrieve something you stole from my people, but you expect me not to get it back? Does that even make sense to you? They are African artifacts, made in Africa and stolen from there."

"Asha, my loyalties are with the United States. I'm just letting you know that if you do anything, I will have no other choice but to take action against you." She seemed aggressive right now. That was one reason Breeden so highly valued her. She knew when to take a stand and when to be the voice of reason. It seemed like this time she was taking a stand.

"I understand that. I won't be doing anything. There is no need to be worried," I lied. I still needed to be sure that these were, in fact, artifacts that belonged to my people. I needed to talk to my brother. "Look, I had a long flight. Why don't I catch up with you tomorrow?" I needed time alone to talk to my brother.

"Sure. You can call me later," she said.

I took the files with the pictures and left.

As soon as I was alone in my room, I snapped pictures of the artifacts and sent them to Femi and I called him. "Did you see the pic-tures I sent you?"

"Looking over them now. These are Ghanaian artifacts. Some of them were taken from the palace years ago during the colonization. At least two of them belong to the Benin nation. Where did you get these pictures?" he asked.

"They called me in to retrieve these. I wanted to confirm if they belonged to us," I said, my head hanging low.

"Now that you know..."

"Nation before self, but how am I supposed to do this?"

"You just answered your question, didn't you?" he said, his voice low.

I heard everything Maya said, but it didn't matter. I wanted to get those artifacts back home, where they belonged. It was my heritage and it would also hold great value to our nation much more than in a museum. More than that, it could help the country unite and help them heal. "I did," I replied after a long pause.

"Do you have the locations of the artifacts?"

Nation before self, I thought before I hit "Send" on another picture I had taken. It was the location of the artifacts. Just hitting Send on that picture was unimaginably hard. I was suffering the same fate Adelaide had. I was facing conflicted loyalties. Even though I was loyal to Ghana, I was still apprehensive. I didn't want to betray the country that had taken me in when I had nowhere else to go, but I also knew that my loyalty to my birth country outweighed everything else. I had chosen this path long ago since I made the decision to help Liberia.

Even if we disregarded that fact, this was one atrocity committed against African countries. Their heritage had been taken from them and they had them displayed in museums for the entertainment of fifth graders who didn't even know what they represented. That was just another form of degradation that could not be overlooked. It was decided. I sent the location of the items to Femi and then cut the call.

I was still looking at the images when I realized that there was no turning back now. It was done, and I couldn't rescind my decision. I kept reminding myself of this just to keep myself convinced. There was nothing left for me to do except wait to meet Maya tomorrow. Without even changing, I got into bed and fell asleep at once.

A day ago, I had been hung up on Jay, and now I was thinking about something different. I guess that was just as much a curse as it was a blessing; given the precious few blessings I've had, I included this on that list. Knowing what I did bothered me, but I convinced myself that being an African was far more important than being an American.

*****

A phone call from Breeden woke me up. I thought I had been asleep for hours, but my phone informed me it had only been half an hour. I picked up the call and immediately knew that something was wrong. "Come in. Now!" he said aggressively.

"Yes, sir," I said and hung up. I got up and went straight to his office.

Upon my arrival, he handed me a file and started talking. "This woman's name is Makayla Edwards. She works for the Department of Defense. Somalian rebels abducted her when she was on a vacation cruise. They had specifically targeted her, trying to get information from her. We need her back ASAP. I already have a team in place, and we have zeroed in on their location. I need you there to lead the team."

I was aware of why he had chosen me. I had an exceptional record with foreign missions, and I'd led them countless times. "What about the artifacts?" I inquired.

"Maya can take care of that. We need to get her back forthwith. Your team is already on stadbywaiting for you. Bring her home." he commanded.

"Will do, sir," I walked into our ops department to get my gear. Within minutes, my team and I were in the air. There were two guys and two girls. They were Special Forces and were all the best at their jobs. I took charge. "Okay, this is a simple operation—infiltrate and extract. Get in the hotel, find her, then get out. First, we need to cut off their power. It'll work to our advantage. Take out everyone who gets in our way. Avoid civilians. You'll know when you see them. Also, we need their leader alive. Do not kill him." I looked at all of them. "We need to know what he knows from his interrogation with the girl."

They all nodded, and for the rest of the ride, we rode silently.
We all had been on missions like
this. We knew how things worked. I was glad to be here rather than with Maya. Even though I was firm on my decision, I still didn't want to see her. It felt as if it fractured the friendship we had.

"Did you get branded, or is that a tattoo? I can't tell," the guy sitting next to me asked.

"A tattoo," I lied. "That's an interesting tattoo to have." he replied.

"Thanks," I said shortly. I meant to get a tattoo to cover up the brand after what the elders did to me but never got the chance.

"Where'd you get it?" he asked.

"Why? Are you going to write a book about it?" I wasn't in the mood to talk to anyone.

118

probably never going to see each other ever again. He got the hint and sat back. The guys spoke amongst themselves, leaving me out of the conversation, and I was glad for it.

After a long ride, the pilot informed us we were about three hundred meters away. "Time to jump," I whispered.

One after another, we all jumped, parachuting close enough to our ground destination. We were miles away from Cairo, but cars were waiting to take us into the city. We scaled the building's side with the least guards and quietly made our way to the power room. Right after we killed the switch that powered the generator, all hell broke loose.

The Exposed

Hearing gunshots, I turned around and saw the guy who had asked me about my mark and three other Somalis were lying dead on the ground. I immediately dove for cover and started shooting. Thankfully, there was still a chance for us to complete our mission. I signaled my team to follow me.

I chose two men from the crew to follow me and ordered the rest to proceed in the opposite direction. "We'll meet back here in five," I said. We cut off the power supply to give us an advantage and began the search to find their leader.

Before we knew it, the opposing side had effortlessly killed the two men guarding the door. I then aimed and started shooting, and bodies started falling like sacks of flour. after we had killed all of them except one, we stopped. "What do you want?" a voice shouted.

"Surrender," I replied.

"I have little choice, do I?" the leader replied. They surrounded him from all sides, and there was no way out. He threw his gun on the ground and we quickly arrested. There was no need to ask him where Makayla was, He told us everything willingly including where Makayla was being held. We got her out and heaed back.

We arrived with no further surprises and got on the armored convoy to transport us back to the naval headquarters. I sent word to Breeden, letting him know Makayla was with me. She needed a change of clothes and some food. There were several cuts on her arms, face, and she was bruised in various other places. She looked like she had been through hell.

I gave her a shirt and a pair of jeans to wear. I remined her we still had a meeting with Breeden before she changed into the clean clothes I gave her. I stood in the mirror staring at the veins on my neck and I rememebered Femi's comment about health and appearance. Before I could have another thought, she gasped. "What's that on your shoulder?" she whispered.

"What?" I asked.

She came closer to me and moved my sir so she could see more clearly. I slapped her hand away from me and moved away. "That is the Royal Mark of Ashanti. You are the queen!" she said and moved away in horror.

I felt a sharp knife cut though my stomach. That was one of my most closely guarded secrets. How could she have possibly known that? The design of the brand given to a queen wasn't common knowledge. Even some people in Ghana wouldn't know what it meant. "What are you talking about?" I said. "This is a tattoo." That was the best explanation I could come up with.

"I am half Ghanaian. I know that mark. I have studied it. There is no way I am wrong about this. You are the queen," she said with complete surety.

"Where have you studied this mark?" I asked.

"I told you. I'm half African. I was born in Cape Coast, and my parents taught me some of our histories. I moved here years ago. How are you even working here?" she asked.

"Makayla, I need you to shut up about this. You can't tell anyone. I will explain everything to you later, Please!

I said. Everything I've done was a hundred percent justified and for the greater good.

"You can't be a spy. You have a kingdom. Why would you be in the Navy?" she said, completely disregarding everything I had said.

"Makayla, I need you to concentrate. I will tell you everything, but you cannot say anything about this in front of Breeden, or there will be irreversible consequences that even I, your queen, cannot withstand." I stressed every word, hoping she would understand just how serious this situation was. "We need to go see Breeden," I said, pulling her after me.

"I will not be a part of your lies." she said.

I just stared at her, wondering if this was it. If this was the day, my entire life would come crashing on me. I had to say something that ease her mind, because if we stayed on this topic any longer, I'd loose my mind. "Makayla, I was born in the Ashanti royal family. I came here because there was a war going on. I came here to save my life. I have done nothing that would make anyone question my loyalty to the United States. I know this is a lot but understand this, I have an excellent reason for being here. I will explain that to you,but for now, just deep this until we cn have a proper chat."

I still wasn't sure if I was safe wih her, but I didn't have a choice. I motioned for her to keep walking, and we made our way to the interrogation room where Breeden was waiting for us. There was no one else in the room except him, and he was looking at the Somali pirate through a one-sided window.

"Good, Asha. You're here. I need you to go in there and ques-tion him. He won't talk with anyone except you. You know the drill."

"Yeah," I said and entered the interrogation room. The prisoner was looking at me, smiling. I was still perplexed about the whole Makayla situation. The United States government had caught him, and he was still sitting there, smiling. He then stretched out his neck as though he was looking past me and opened his mouth to say something, but his entire expression changed to that of outrage and shock.

"*Nana Nyankupon*," he whispered in Twi. Meaning, "Oh my god," and I froze where I stood. "I can't believe my eyesight," he said in a calm voice, and it completely took me off guard. What the hell was he talking about? I couldn't even answer him in Twi. I played dumb.

"This is America. Speak English," I said, putting up my best effort to pretend.

"You can't even speak your native language in front of them can you?

I knew two things for sure. Even if I continued not to understand anything else he was saying, one ing w certain; we both knew who I really was. He was going to use it to his advantage. Filled with rage, I rushed out of the room and went back into the office. Breeden followed me. "What is he talking about? What language is he speaking?

"I think it was some African language. Twi mybe?"

"So we need a translator. Then we can understand what hes's saying."

"No, wait. He'll give in. No need to get a translator. I'm sure Makayla told you everything anyways. I dont think he know much," I was scared to death what would happend if yet another person got involved. I needed to stall. I still didn't have any idea how I was going to get out of this situation.

"Makayla told me she revealed nothing. She said you guys rescued her in time. But we still need to know what he's saying, so we need a translator," Breeden replied.

"He speaks English. There's no need to get a translator. He will talk, and we'll get what we need." Even if we got him a translator, he would probably not say anything but I couldnt afford that. Prehaps killing him wasn't such a bad idea after all. He knew entirely too much.

I had aleady confessed to Makayla to keep her quiet, If anything were to happen to him, she would suspect me. There was a solution to all of this. *Kill both of them*, I thought, but I could never do that. I needed Jay, my brother, or mom—someone!

Being the queen of Ashanti was forcing me to walk down a dark path, a path that was making me keep secrets and do things I wasn't proud of. Making morally questionable decisions was something that I had been doing for a long time, but now it wasn't because somebody else ordered me to. I was in control, and I was scared beyond belief. I'm afraid where this path could lead me.

I was considering going through with killing this idiot, but I couldn't figure out how much it would change me. I couldn't do that just yet, Makayla was still in the picture, and I had to take care of that first.

"All right. I'll have the guards take him to his cell. You can take another shot at him whenever you want." I've asked Makayla all I needed to. She must report back to her office tomorrow." he said kindly looking at Makayla.

I looked over at her and remembered I had promised to tell her everything and the though of that was driving me crazy.

"Yeah, you're right. I need to go home and take a shower. I'll go to get to them work." Makayla said, finally looking at me.

That was about the best I could hope for. I nodded back, and we all took off. There was nothing left to do, and even though I had just been to Cairo and back, I didn't feel the least bit tired. Contrarily, I felt nothing, but I knew with what had happened, I was in no condition to go home. I had left my phone and everything else in my office, so I went back and sat down. I took out my phone and saw that I had missed two calls from Femi. I didn't want to talk to him in this environment, so I took off.

*****

I called him after I reached home. "Hey, you called?" I asked. "Yeah, where were you?"

"I was on a mission. We had a somewhat rescue mission. She's fine now," I said. I wasn't in the mood to talk or tell anyone anything. On the surface, I appeared fine. One of the many advantages of being a master of your own emotions. "Why did you call?"

"I just wanted to tell you we had a meeting with the elders. They were infuriated, they will do nothing fo now." he aded.

"That's a relief. Thanks."

"Yeah, Mom misses you. I'll tell her you said hi. She'll feel better."

"Ha ha. Sure. Look, I need to go. Keep me updated," I said and hung up. I sat down on my bed and tried to think about what I needed to do. Hopelessly, my mind came up with nothing. It was a total blank except for one thought: *I need to talk to Makayla.* That was on top of the priority list, so I made a few calls to get her home address and took off. I thought about what I would say. All I could do right was to see what questions she asked and answer them truthfully. My life was in complete chaos.

I stood on her doorstep and knocked. She must have been waiting for me because she immediately opened her door. "Come in," she said.

125

I was about to step inside her house and decided against it. I dont need anyone listening to my conversations. "Why don't we sit in my car?"

"Why?"

"It's just safer." I said, trying to get my point across without saying it.

"Sure," she reluctantly agreed and followed me.

I unlocked my car and climbed in. "Ask me anything."

"Who else knows?" She wasn't wasting any time.

"In totality, three people who alswork with me. I can't tell you who they are,"

"Why are you working here? Don't you have a kingdom to return to?"

" I still have another two years on my contract."

"How do I know you're not copromised?"

"I said I'd give you answers not explanations, and to be clear, I am no and have never been compromised. I do my job exceptionally well. Why would I come back to work here when I have an entire army and a nation to protect me?"

"Because you need intel. I had been thinking about it. The Liberian attack. You could have had a hand in it."

"I'm not Liberian. It had nothing to do with me. Why would I need to orchestrate that?"

"What information was stolen?"

"If you need to ask, then you don't need to know." I said shortly.

"Fair enough," she said, looking at her hands.

"Anything else?"

"Look, I need to ask you a huge favor," she said, still refusing to meet my eyes.

That was something I had not considered, that there could be something she needed that I could use to compensate for her. "What is it?"

"I need to disappear."

It was like someone had taken the oxygen out of my lungs. "You need to do what?" I asked

"You heard me," she said, looking at me.
"Why do you want to disappear?" I can't allow anything like this ever to happen again. I am broken, Asha. They tortued me." She lifted her shirt and showed me her scars. They had burned her, cut her, and bruised her all over. Her skin was still blood red. "I don't want to do this any longer, and I wont be able to escape them unless I am gone for good."

"You signed up for this. You knew the associated risks didn't you?" I asked.

"It's different knowing that something can happen and atually having it happen to you. Tell me, have you ever been through anything like this?" she asked quietly.

"Do you need to ask me that. You know who I am and
what I've been through." I said.

"I have a choice, and so do you. I want out. You can get out if want. You can make that happen."

I thought about what she said. I had never considered that statement. *You always have a choice.* I thought about lying on a beach somewhere, relaxing with Jay by my side. We would get up and walk, his fingers interlaced in mine, without the responsibility of Ashanti on me, without the tension of breaking my contract, and without having to worry about anything.

Some people thought dealing with problems was the way to feel alive. They didn't know the resst of us who dealt with issues all their lives want a moment of peace. For us, it was like problems were always lined up one by one. Solved one? Here, you get two more. I would give anything to feel like myself again, without the tension and anxiety. I wanted to break down and cry, laugh to my heart's fulfillment, and dance all with Jay and yet I couldn't. I just wanted to feel normal.

Just about anything was better than this numbness. I thought about my father and how he had to make tough choices throughout his life. I thought about Femi, who was back on my side suporting me. I thought about my mother, who stood by my side, always reminding me of my duties. But mostly, I thought about the people of Ashanti, who needed a leader to rule them. They had lived most of their lives in poverty, suppressed by foreigners, enslaved, and out-casts in their nation. I had lived a privileged life in comparison to them. This very moment was why my father made sure I suvived to take care of my people.

Every girl who died during the civil war years ago, I owed. Everyone of them who didn't make it—I owed. The debt was to be settled, and I hadn't yet done that yet. I was going to settle this debt, even if it took me all my life. Reflecting on our conversation, I turned my attention back to her. "We are not talking about me. We are talking about you," I said, masking my emotions yet again.

"I don't want to live this life any longer. I want to live a normal life, but I can never do that unless I have a new identity. You know this. You are never free of this life and this country, and they will never let you be free. Please, I beg you," she pleaded.

I looked at her and saw a broken spirit. It reminded me of myself. I was convinced. I was going to help her. This life wasn't for her. She would never survive. Her situation made me think of myself. I wished so dearly I dared to choose myself above all and abandon my duties. I hoped that I had someone to rescue me from my traditional afflictions. I thought, *If someone could offer me a way out, I would take it*. The cisions I was forced to make lately was changing me. "I'll help you. Don't worry," I said.

At that moment, I wasn't worried if she was going to expose me. I wanted to give her an out. Maybe it was because I saw myself in her. If I couldn't escape my problems, at least I could help her escape hers.

The Maiden

Makayla got out of the car and went back into her house. I didn't have the willpower to drive away imediately. That conversation had taken a lot out of me. It made me aware of some apsects of my situation I hadn't bother to consider. Even still, I pushed the thoughts aside and focused on what I had promised her. I was confident I could deliver on my word and get her a new identity, but it wouldn't be easy. I knew just the right person to call.

"Hello, brother," I said when Femi picked up the call.

No matter what he did, the best thing about him was that he would always answer the call. "Hey, sis. How's everything going?"

"Everything is collapsing Femi."

From the other end, I heard an outburst of laughter and I joined him. It felt good to look at so many problems in the face and laugh. I mean what else couldI do?

"Haha!" he said, still laughing. "Can't a brother assume that his sister just wants to talk about the weather when she calls?" Femi asked.

"When your sister also is the queen of Ashanti, it is best not to assume that," I said lightheartedly.

"So what can I do for you?" Femi asked me.

I had no idea how I would explain the situation to him over the phone. There wasn't exactly a blueprint for conversations like this one. "Okay, so the thing is, I went on that rescue mission, and the girl we rescued saw my mark

130

the elders gave me. She recognized who I was and confronted me about it. and I made sure she wouldn't say anything for now. But as It turns out, She wants something in return. She wants a new identity. I think being taken took a toll on her. She want to disappear and she needs my help."

Pausing, I heard Femi take in a deep breath beore he spoke. "Do you honestly think it's a good idea to get involved?"

"What are you worried about?" I asked. Femi confirmed he was thinking along the same lines I had in the back of y mind. "What if she can't be trusted? What if you do this for her, and she still outs you? What if she wants to go away from all of this, but someone finds out about it and holds that against you? You are already crossing enough lines as it is," Femi warned.

He didn't mean any offense by it, and I didn't take any. I was obliterating almost every line the former rulers of Ashanti had followed and my elders were sick of me. *My situation is different.* I kept telling myself.

"If the elders found out about this, I'm not sure they will let you continue any of this. I'm just saying there are a lot of risks involved," he added.

"I know the risks involved, and I know just what lines I'm crossing," I said. "But the thing is, I can't go back on my word. I already told her I would help her. I trust my instincts."

When I told Makayla I would help her out, It was beacuse trusted her. I don't believe she will betray me. I saw what those Somalian rebels could do and had done to her. It's real.

"Sis, if you trust her, then so do I," Femi said.
"Good. There's one more thing I need to tell you," I said before Femi could go on.

"What's that?"

"The rebel we freed Makayla from, he also knows that I'm the queen. He was speaking to me in Twi in front of my spervisor ."

Femi took another deep breath. "What? Where is he being held?" It was apparent that he was thinking.

"In a cell, here in the States," I answered. Since our childhood, Femi had always tred to protected me from everything, and this situation was no different.

"Okay. This is serious. I need to get on the first flight to you. We need to resolve this issue immediately. I have contacts over there. I'll help you find thegirl her a new identity and deal with the prisoner." He concluded.

Femi had spent the better part of his life in Ashanti ben raised as the fure King of his people. It made sense he knew people who had immense resources at their disposal.

"Yes, I think it's time you visited me. But you can't let any-one know you're coming, except the elders. I don't care about them finding out. They probably think you're coming to bail me out of something."

"Asha, I know the elders come down hard on you, but I need you to know they aren't as wise as they think they are. You are the one who has aways looked out for me. I was making one terrible choice after the next. I'll make sure they know why I am coming there." I felt a rush of affection for my brother. It was long overdue.

I missed the feeling of knowing someone understood me. I had Maya, Adelaide, and Jay in the past, but they never completely understood what it meant to be the Queen of the Ashanti people. "Femi," I said after gathering my thoughts to express the affection I felt for him, "thank you."

"Don't bother at all." Femi replied. "I'll be coming shortly. I'll call an emergency meeting and talk to the elders. In te meantime, I'll give mum heads up."

"Okay, that's perfecct." I said.

"Well, lots of work to do and not enough time. Hopefully, I'll be seeing you soon baby siste. Take care!" Femi ended the call in excietment and it felt like nothing had happened between us. We were back to our usual selves, I had completely forgiven him for everything.

He deserved that much from me. "See you soon, brother. I ishpered to myself as I ended the call on my end.

Talking to him put my mind to ease. Feeling hungry, I got in my car and stopped by the nearest pizzeria, then went straight to my apartment and crashed. That was the first time in a long time I had a good night's sleep.

*****

Waking up the next day, I felt refreshed, rather than feeling exhausted. I laid in bed for the better at of the day, partly waiting on Femi and partly plotting on what I needed to do. Femi had contacts in the States; he helped me find smeone to get Makayla a new identity. I freshened quickly and made my way to meet her.

Fem was in town. I texted him the address to my place so he could stay over. I knocked and waited for her to open the door when I got to her place. She was drssed, ready to step out. "Hey, I need to talk to you," I said.

"Did you make any headway?" she asked with eyes wide and hopeful.

"I did. Are you going out?" I asked her in return.
"Breeden wants to have me questioned yet again abouthe incident. I can reschedule, I don't want to go over there anyway." she said.

Breeden was thorough. I understood why the repetition of her story was crucial. "No, it's best if you go. Stick to whatever you've already told them. It's important to show them you fully intend to continue working there. Otherwise, they will get suspicious."

What Makayla needed me to do tough. I couldnt afford anything joepardizing this mission.

"I suppose you're right. I'll probably be over there for an hour. You can pick me up after? We'll talk then!"

"That's fine. I'll just wait for you in the car." After her meeting was over, I decided to check in with Breeden and get some update on our prisoner. "Makayla, why don't I take you home? I'll come by and check on you later. I need to take care of some things first" I told her.

"That's fine," she said.

I could sense she had something on her mind and I so wanted her to keep it to herself, but I coldn't help it. "What is it?" I asked.

"What are you going to do about the prisoner?" she wondered "I don't know for sure, but I can't let him say anything about who I am to anyone."

"There is only one way to achieve that, you know."
Makayla said suspiciously.

It shocked me to hear her say this, but I wanted to confirm she was saying what I thought she was saying. "What are you talking about?"

"You know what I'm talking about. Don't tell me you aren't thinking the same thing."

"I haven't had any thoughts about anything." I lied. I needed her to say it God knows because I couldn't.

"You need to kill him yourself or have him killed." she said plainly, and I instantly pulled over. I couldn't believe what she was saying. "That's the only way that your identity stays a secret. There is no guarantee that he will keep quiet about this. He has no motivation to live. These people don't look at death like we do. They aren't afraid of it."

The torture they had inflicted on her had completely changed her perspective on life. "It's my problem, not yours. I'll take care of it how I see fit," I said, putting an end to the conversation. I may have agreed to help her but we weren't friends. I dropped her off at the Pentagon. I went to the naval headquarters and straight into Breeden's office.

"Asha, what can I do for you?" Breeden asked after I greeted him.

"I wanted to get an update on the prisoner," I said shortly.

"Well, they have transported him to Florence," he told me.

"You sent him to the federal prison?"

"Yes. We still don't know what kind of intel he has, and there has been no word from the prison, so he clerly still hasn't said a word." Breeden said.

I conviced myself there was nothing to worry about. "Okay, sir. Thank you. Keep me updated, please." It made sense for me to be kept in the loop about it, as I was the one who brought him in.

"If anything comes up, I'll let you know."

I understood myself to be dismissed after he assured me. After talking with Breeden, I went out into my car and called Femi. He had texed me earlier that he was almost here and I needed to make sure he was okay.

"Hey, sis."

"Hey, where are you?"

"I'm here already. I am waiting for you at your house."

"On my way."

I wanted to talk to Femi first, to discuss the details of getting her a new identity before we got to Makayl's house. I sent her a message to prepare for our arrival and sped home to my brother.

*****

Femi was waiting for me in my room. Seeing him made me so happy I couldn't explain my joy. He got up and hugged me as tightly as he could. "I missed you, brother," I whispered.

"I missed you too, and so does Mother.

It wouldn't kill you tocall her every now and then you know."

135

"Haha! Sure. That lady talks too much. Plus I'm avoiding her this time. I can't have any tals of marriage right now."

He moved away and looked at me. "You are getting thinner by the second, you know. You look unwell."

" Can he tell what's going on with me? I ccan't afford for anyone to know the secrets that hanted me admist all of this drama." I thought and looked at myself in the mirror. He was right. I had been having a hard time keeping food down these days and I had an idea what the reason could be. "Well, that's wt happens when you're stressed." I said, and we both laughed.

"So when are we meeting this person who wants to disappear?"
"We will. But first, what is the plan?"

"I know someoe who can do it, but his methods are crude," Femi said distastefully. "He vanishes people completely for a living. He's very good at his job."

"How do you know him?"
"I found out about him through the general."
"I didn't tell him why I needed to know, and he didn't ask," Femi clarified.
"Tell me more about this man."
"Well, he goes by the name Joe. I know how to contact him. He's been doing this for about forty years. He sets up a scene that makes the authority sure that the person who wants to disappear has died. They can investigate it to the bone and do what they wish, but they will never suspect anything. After that, he moves the person to another country of their choosing, and they can continue living their life normally as if nothng;s happened." he explained. "The way he sets up the scene—that's the main issue because he uses dead bodies and blood samples to ensure that the authorities can investigate as much as they like without finding out the truth."

"You said he uses dead bodies. Where does he get them?" I'm not okay with someone loosing their life so Makayla could get her freedom."

"That is something only he knows," Femi replied. "I've never acquired his sevices so I'm not sure how he operates. That may be our ony option given who he works for. We can't afford to make any mistakes. Bringing in Joe is be our best shot."

"For her to disappear completely?"

"I believe so."

"Okay, then. No need to wase aymore time," I said.

"I think I'll freshen up first before we go meet her."

"Sure. "

After he had gotten ready, we headed to Makayla's place.

*****

" Makayla, this is Femi, my brother. He has a plan to get you out."

Femi explained the process to her. Makayla nodded in agreement "Do you have any idea how long this will take?" she asked after considering what Femi had told her.

"That is something that Joe can tell us," Femi told her. "I don't want to give you any inaccurate information."

"I just want to get this over with as soon as possible, please. At he meting today, I could feel they didn't trust me. I don'tt think they believe I kept my mouth shut. There's no telling what they will do to me." she said.

She was close to tears, and I felt sorry for her. Her tears were useless. What she needed was therapy, but even those sessions could be overthrown in the name of national security. I couldn't have her spilling any information about me. So, instead of suggesting therapy, I kept my mouth shut. "We'll do whatever we can to speed up the process. Don't worry," I said.

"Femi, how do we contact this person?" I asked him.

"I have a number," he said and pulled out a piece of paper.

He called the number and set up a meeting for us. We were to meet at a hote close by my house in an hour. Femi and I went back to my place to pick up a few things, and then we headed to the hotel.

*****

We arrived fifteen minutes early. There was a knock at the door. He looked like a gentleman. By looking at him, I wouldn't have guessed this was is profession. Femi told me he had been in the business for about forty years, but he didn't look a day over thirty-five. He had a close-cropped military-style cut, and I wondered if he had served prior. He wore a black suit and a tie. He looked like an off-duty general, heavily built with a deep-set face and piercing gray eyes. Knowing this, I realized we were in a room with a danger-ous man, and I didn't like it. I had promised Makayla I would help, there was no going back on my word.

The plan I had in mind left no room for error, so hopefully, he knew what he was doing. I stepped aside and let him in. "Hello, Femi, Asha," he said nodding toward us. That made me even more nervous than I was before. "Who told him my name?

"I do like to know the people I'm conducting business with. In your case, the general. He's a good man! He contacted me as soon as you told him." he said, pointing toward Femi.

"How do you know the general?" I asked him.

"He and I go way back. I was in Ghana on a mission much like this one. It turns out I was doing business with some very powerful and bad people. They didn't want any loose ends and decided I was just that, so they planned to have me killed. Your father found out about it but wanted to keep his involvement hidden. My hope was lost until your father sent the general to rescue me. He was the best of your men, you know," he spoke candidly. "I promised both the general and your father that if they ever needed my services, I would be glad to help them. I'm here to settle a debt," he finished.

Femi and I exchanged a glance. We knew then that we could trust him. "I see," I said. "Why don't you come in, and we'll give you more details on what's going on."

Femi began to explain the situation concerning Makayla. After we had finished talking, he looked at us strangely. He asked me some questions about her, and I answered as best as I could. "So why you are helping this woman?" he asked me.

"Because I want her to disappear. She knows who I am, and her disappearance works best for both of us." I said, but Joe didn't seem convinced.

"Compassionate much, queen?" he asked.

"That is none of your business," Femi interjected. "As you said, you are here to settle a debt. Please do that."

Joe looked at Femi and smiled. "Well, you are the son of your father. He too was quick to anger, but I suppose you are right."

"How will you be doing it?" I asked him.

"That's my problem. But since you will have a problem with my usual methods, I was thinking of arson." He saw the confusion my face and continued. "Let me paint you a picture. Makayla is in her house and there's a gas leak that causes a fire. But she's asleep so she doesn't notice, and the entire house burns down. When the fire department arrives, they put out the fire but cannot salvage the house. They go in just to find a body on the floor burned beyond recognition. They conduct a postmortem to confirm the victim and do so using the victim's blood and tooth or two. They find out it's her's and case closed. Meanwhile, Makayla is on her way to a country of her choice with a new identity."

"Where are you going to get a body?"

"This is Washington, Asha. There's bodies everywhere. I'm sure we can find one that looks somewhat like Makayla," he said nonchalantly.

"If you think you're going to set someone on fire and burn them just to get this job done then think again!" No matter how much I wanted to help,there were boundaries I still couldn't cross.

"Asha, I have never killed an innocent person in my life and I won't start now. Femi and I will discuss the details of what I need from her to make this happen." I nodded in agreement.

I was glad to be spared the details. *The things I have to endure.* I thought. "As long as you don't kill someone."

"I suppose we should meet Makayla now."

The Chaos

I introduced Makayla to Joe and assured her she was in excellent hands.

Femi and I went back to my place. I was about to get out of the car, but Femi stopped me. "Why don't you go on? I'll catch up with you later." I became confused.

"Why? Where do you have to go?"

"I told Adelaide I would meet with her, so I'm going to her place."

"Since when are you and Adelaide friends? You two hated each other," I yelled as I recalled the many times, she had gotten into a dispute with him.

"We made up a few days before you were crowned queen. We stopped talking after the attack on Liberia, but I called her again after we settled our isues. She didn't want to, but I convinced her to stay in touch after I apologized."

I could tell he wasn't sincere. "Why didn't you tell me?" I questioned.

"Was there any reason to?"

"Femi, why are you getting defensive?" I trusted Femi, and I trusted Adelaide, but I also knew that if they were to get involved, the consequences would be damning.

"I am not getting defensive, and I could ask you why are you asking so many questions?"

"Because you don't seem to understand the consequences of you two getting involved," I said.

When he raised his eyebrows, I continued, "Look, Adelaide is in the military, and if you two get involved and things get serious, she may have to answer questions about you, and that will inadvertently reveal my identity and open our tribe alot more problems than we need. She won't choose you over her country."

"Whoa! First, nobody said anything about choosing anybody. Second, I'm an adlt, and it's not that serious. But just so you know, while I am staying here, I will stay with her," he said.

"What!" I didn't mean to yell.

"Well, in the spirit of total honesty, I suppose you should know," he said, smiling.

"Femi, what are you doing?" I held up my hand. "Don't tell me. I don't wanna know. Just go, but you're not taking my car."

"I don't need your car. I'm a prince," he replied cockily. He got out of the car and got in another vehicle parked right outside my house and sped away. I was left alone staring after him. Where did he even get a car from? *Wow*, I thought.

I entered my house, and before I could even put my phone down, it rang. Breeden calls always made me nervous. Maybe the pirate had told him I was the queen. I decided to at least talk to him before continuing to make any more assumptions. "Yes, sir?" I said, picking up the call.

"Come into my office now," he said and hung up the call. I got back in my car and drove to his office.

When I arrived at his office, he was sitting, waiting for me. That was unusual. Usually, he would do some work, and his table would be a mess of confidential documents, but it seemed like there was something important that he wanted to talk about. "Asha, come in. Sit," he told me before I had even saluted him.

I tried to remain calm and sat down. "Everything okay, sir?" I asked.

"Not really, no. I have just received some disturbing information about you," he said.

It was like I heard his voice from far away like somebody had pulled the ground out from under my feet. It was good that I was sitting down for this because my knees would probably have buckled if not. "Really? From whom?" Even though I was trembling underneath, I didn't want to let any of it show on my face.

"That's not important, but the allegations made are disturbing."

"Sir, what is going on?"

"It was alleged that you are the queen of the Ashanti Region in Ghana. The previous ruler, who was your father, died, and you were made the queen instead of your brother."

I needed to handle this with much diligence. One mistake, a slight inconsistency in my story, and the consequences would be so huge. "So you say that I am the queen of Ashanti?"

"I didn't say it. It was alleged," he replied, staring at me.

"Sir, no offense, but you realize just how far-fetched that is, right? How would I be the queen of Ashanti? Surely, the person who told you this must have backed his claim with proof, right?"

"They did."

He opened his laptop and played a video clip of me on the day of my coronation. It was blurred. The way I was dressed and the makeup I had on in the video made it hard to discern if it was me.

After the clip ended, I looked at Breeden. "You think that's me?"

"Again, I did not."

"I know you didn't say that it was me, but I'm asking if you think that's me."

"What I think is not important. It is important what you say regarding this allegation and why someone would do this."

It relieved me. If he were convinced it was me, we wouldn't be having a conversation about it. He asked me about this. He was begging me to tell him what was going on because he wasn't sure. "I am not the queen of Ashanti." I lied through my teeth, and it made my skin crawl. "If we are talking about why someone would do this, I have no idea."

"This is a huge deal, and if we put you in the same clothes this woman is wearing, you two would look similar to me." He wasn't completely satisfied with the answer I'd given.

"Sir, I don't get it. Are you calling me a liar?"

"I am just pointing out the obvious."

"Would you like me to get in this dress for you to compare us?" I asked him, smiling.

"This isn't a joke, Asha."

"It sure seems like one to me. Why would I even be sitting here if I had an entire country at my disposal?"

"Spy," he replied shortly.

"Seems excessive, don't you think? Look, sir, I have already told you that's not me, and I have also told you I don't know why anyone would claim otherwise."

"When you have eliminated the impossible, whatever remains, however improbable, must be the truth." Breeden smiled slightly. "The simplest explanation of why someone would claim this is because it is, in fact, you."

I looked at Breeden, shocked. I couldn't believe what he was saying, but then it hit me. "Are you kidding me?"

"Asha, this is a serious allegation. I don't think you are the Ashanti queen, but this woman looks an awful lot like you. I'll see what happens. For now, you are free to go, but keep in mind, if I have this, you can safely assume that everyone else in this department does too. I have to let the higher-ups know."

I just smiled and left. *Who the hell could've sent that video? Could it have been the prisoner who told them about this?* He couldn't have gotten his hands on that video in prison. I didn't want to think about it, but my suspicion went directly to Femi. He had betrayed me in the past, but ever since I had told him why I was crowned queen, he had been entirely loyal to me. Yet I was convinced there wasn't anyone else who could have done this.

*****

I went back to my house and sat on my bed. I was still suspicious of Femi, so I called Maya and Adelaide to talk to them. I could handle just about anything in my life, but this was too much, even I had my limits. Suppose my true identity had gotten out to the States. I didn't even want to think about what would happen then, but I knew it wouldn't be something that Ghana could recover from. I called Maya and asked her to bring Adelaide with her to my house. When they came in, I told them about what Breeden had said.

"Shit. What are you going to do now?" Maya asked.

"I have handled the situation for now, but I still have no idea who could have possibly sent in that intel," I said untruthfully. And both of them exchanged a look.

"Who do you suspect?" Adelaide asked.

"Femi. He had pretended to be on my side before and ended up betraying me." I looked at Adelaide. If I was going to talk about this, then I might as well speak bravely.

"You think it was...?" Adelaide trailed off. "It couldn't be him," she said, shaking her head. "He is loyal to you."

"Anything is possible. The clip he showed me was taken from a news channel in Ghana. The only people who know about who I work for are you guys, Femi, my mom, and the elders. I know you guys didn't do this. My mom wouldn't do this, and neither would the elders. That leaves Femi. Nobody else knows."

It made sense, and I felt torn. How could Femi do this to me? After everything else we'd been through, how could he betray me? I had handled the situation for now, but I knew there would be a full investigation.

"He wouldn't do this, Asha. He is loyal to you," Adelaide repeated herself.

"Adelaide, I know about you guys, so I'm not surprised you're defending him, but he betrayed me recently. How am I to be sure it wasn't him this time?"

"What?" Maya exclaimed.

"You're dating her brother?" She looked directly at Adelaide.

"Well, it's not like—"

" I knew it! From the first day you saw him at the air-port."
She was smiling.

"Anyway," Adelaide dramatized as she rolled her eyes. "there's
only one way to be sure." Ash said and took out her phone.

"What are you doing?"

"Texting him. We need to get to the bottom of things"

I snatched the phone away from her. "You are doing no such
thing," I told her.

"Well, how are you going to be sure it was him then?"

I couldn't go back home to get my own answers, but I knew
someone who could. "I can have the general investigate." I said.

"Asha, you need to talk to him first," she replied.
"Adelaide, I think your feelings are getting the best of you."

"It isn't. I know Femi, and he wouldn't do this," she said.

"You don't," I said. "Look, don't say a word about this to him.
I will ask the general to investigate. If nothing turns up, then I will
talk to him. If there is something, then we will know. But do not
tell him, okay?"

She hesitated for a bit and then finally responded "Okay."
"What is going on between you and Femi, anyway?" Maya
asked.

"He's in town , and he's staying with me."

"So you guys are official now?"

"No, not really," Adelaide said with a side glance to me.

I pretended not to notice as I dialed the generals number.
I told him about the entire situation, and he promised to get back to
me with some answers.

I hung up the call and turned toward them. It felt a sense of
déjà

vu. The only person missing was Jay, and even though so much was going on, I still missed him deeply. I was trying to keep my composure, but Maya noticed my uneasiness.

"Asha, is everything okay?" I wanted to break down, but I couldn't so I just I told them what had happened between him and I.

"How in the hell could they make you marry some other guy?" Adelaide said, outraged.

"It is the custom for the Ashanti ruler to marry someone within our tribe. I can't do anything about it." My heart was racing as I spokethose words

"That is a dumb tradition. You and Jay belong together," Adelaide said.

I wanted to yell "I know!" but I refrained, opting to smile instead. "Well, it is what it is," I said.

"You're right, Asha," Maya said as she hugged me. "It's going to be okay. You are the queen. Some sacrifices must be made."

She was trying to make me feel better, and I was thankful to her for at least trying to understand.

"Yeah, I know." "But I don't think you should get married right away," Maya said thoughtfully. "You may pretend right now that you are fine, but you won't e able to love again until you've healed from what happened with Jay."

"I need to make a call." I said finally understanding what she meantdialing my mother's number. "Hey, Mom."

"Hello, Asha. How are you?"

I could sense an underlying worry in her voice. "I'm good and you?"

"I'm fine. Is everything okay?"

"I need you to talk to the elders. I can't come just yet. I am being deployed again and I won't be able to return for some time. I need you to handle the elders, okay?"

It bothered me lying to her, but I knew this was the only chance I had to get my emotions sorted out with Jay.

"I can do that. When will Femi be coming home?"

"I don't know yet. I still need him here. I'll let you know if any-thing chnges."

"Sure. Take care, Asha," she replied and hung up.

The Imprisoned

"Hey, Mom, what's up?"

Maya and Adelaide had just left my house, and I was prepared to step out. It was a little unusual for her to call at this hour so I hoped all was well.

"I wanted to ask if you knew where Jay is," she asked

That's weird, I thought. I hadn't spoken to him since the last time we talked."You all made me dump him remember?" I wondered why my mother even cared. This was all her fault anyway.

I'd just spoken to her recently and she didn't bother to ask then. "I have no idea where he is. Why do you ask?" I hoped he hadn't gotten himself into any trouble.

"Well, it aars he's back in Kumasi. I just got a report from the general. He told me Jay came into the country aboutwo weeks ago. He's been spending time in the village and helping ou the community."

I had no idea what to make of this. What was he planning to do?

"Turns out, he's popular among the villagers. They are calling him *modof* (my beloved). Our people like him a lot. He's even won the heart of some elders. I didn't know where she was even going with this. Why was she telling me this? Did this mean that I could marry Jmarry and live hapily? or was she telling me to cause more pain. Being reminded I

149

couldn't have the life I wanted made me angry all over. This Isn't what I needed right now. "Wait, did you say he's now familiar with the elders?"

"Yes, most of them like him a lot."
I smiled. "Why are you telling me this?" I asked her

"I just thought you should know. He was staying in a guesthouse not far away from the palace, but it was reported that he has gone. I asked the general to see what he could find about hs disappearance, and he tolthe Americans ordered his immediate arrest and took him."

I could sense she wasn't the least bit worried about Jay and it made my blood boil. "When did this happen?" I asked through gritted teeth.

"About a week ago."
"I see. I'll find out what happened." I didn't want to talk to her anymore.Thhe insincerity in her tone provoked me. "Listen, Mom, I have to go. I'll call you later."

What was I supposed to do? I had no way of knowing what acally happened, prepahps I knew someone who might. If what my mother had told me was true, Jay was probably back in the States and in trouble.Breeden certainly would've known about it. First, I needed to figure out who exposed me to him. For his sake, I hope it wasnt Femi. He was my brother, but if he had betrayed me yet again, I would feed his beating heart to our gods.

There was just no way around it. I had less than six hours before receiving a call from the general with some information regarding this betrayal, and there was nothing I could do but wait. I thought about why Jay had gone to Kumasi and why was he doing charity work without telling me. What was his agenda? Maybe he hoped I was still in Kumasi? but that didn't explain why he would stay there. Nothing mae sense.

*****

After what seemed like hours of lying still in my bed, I cam up with a theory that made somewhat sense.Maybe it was Breeden who gave the orders to have everyone close to me investi-gated. He had been my CO for the longest time, and he knew whom I was close. He had Jay takn for sure! I got out of bed and immediately went to Jay's apartment. From the outside, it looked fine. If what I thought was true, I would have to be careful of what I as about to do next.

I had exactly fifteen seconds to get into his house withou being noticed y his cameras. I had already scoured the street up and down for any cars that looked suspicious and didn't find any. I looked into the apartment, and it confirmed my fears. The entire house had been turned upside down. Iknew exactly wht tey might have been looking for; anything that connected him to me. Our pictures—damn! I got out of the doorway and ran into his room.The pictures were gone. Damn! They had taken him on either the orders of Breeden or someone even higher up the chain.

I had to do something! I would have to tell the truth! What the hell was I supposed to do? On one hand, I had a country to protect. on he other, I couldn't leave Jay like that. Wht could I possibly even say to Breeden.

I was pacing back and forth and could feel my brain trying to tear itself apart. In training, they teach us the importance of sacrifice and loyalty. Jay needed me. I couldn't fail him. I dialed the general's number. "Have any information on Femi yet?" I asked him.

"My queen, I told you I would need at least a day. It has barely been ten hours," he replied. "I've found nothing. I'm already run out of leads. If he sent the intel to Breeden, he did it well because there's no evidence of it. I am sorry, my queen."

"Don't be. That's good news. I hoped you wouldn't. I need you to trace Jelani's phone. Will you be able to do that?"

"If it was the Americans who took him, it maybe a little hard to locate him. Let me see what I can do. I'll let you know if I have something." he said.

"Okay, sure. Thanks!"
I was glad the general hadn't found anything connecting Femi to this betrayal. It was safe to say it wasn't him, and I was thankful for it because I needed him.

I drove over the back to Adelaide's house and knocked on her door. "Asha, what are you doing here?" she asked.

"Have you spoken to Breeden?" I asked and walked in.

"What? No."

"Check your phone for bugs," I said poiting to her phone and noticd Femi walkng up towards us. I instruced him to do the same thing. They looked at me as if I had completely lost my mind. I took them outside, and we sat in my car. I explained to them Jay had been abducted or arrested on the orders of either Breeden or someone else higher ranking than Breeden. I calmed my nerves as tried to finish explaining what I saw at Jay's house and laid out my suspicions.

"So you came here to check to see wht exactly?" Adelaide questioned.

"I needed to make sure you and Femi were safe. Femi," I looked at him. "I think you need to go back to Ghana. If you get caught with her, it will become too big of an issue to handle."

"Asha, I'm staying herefor now," he replied stubbornly.

"Fine, let's go to Maya's then," I said and started my car. I was in no mood for arguments. We got to Maya's house and I heard my phone ringing. It was a call from Breeden and my heart began racing. I looked at Adelaide, then Femi. She motioned me to pick up the call.

"Asha, in my office, now!" he yelled quickly hung up.

I was anxious. This may be the first genuine lead I would have on Jay. "I'm going. I'll call you when I'm done." They were about to say something but I immediately put up my hands. "I don't have time. I need to leave."

They nodded, and I sped off. I practically ran to his office. He was sitting in his chair, looking overly concerned. "Sit down and tell me the truth Asha, Are you or are not the reigning queen of the Ashanti people in Ghana?"

I went blank. His question formed a block of ice down my throat and into my stomach. I had already lied to him once, and I couldn't go back on my word, so I lied again. "I've already answered that questioned. Now, you tell me this, Where is Jelani?" On my way here, I had thought about how I was going to have this conversation.

"How do you know about Jelani?" he asked "I went to his house. He wasn't there, it was completely torn apart." "That wasn'tan answer to my question."

"Asha, can you say you've given me an honest answer to my question?" We were both clearly infuriated with eachother, Yet remained calm, fully aware of my lies.

"How about you tell me where Jelani is?"
"We took him while he was in Kumasi. near your palace. Since then, He's being held for interrogation."

"Jay refuses to say anything about your status and heritage in Ghana. That's what I was told. They refused to hand over the recordings of the interrogation. He told me to let you know he's okay and asked me to keep you safe. Asha, what the he is going on?"

Being that teling the truth may now be my only option to save Jay, I told him everythin.g "A long time ago, there was a civil war in my country, which resulted in me needing to run. Years later, I was made queen because of a prophecy instead of my brother. So yes, I am the queen,"

Life's were at stake and knowing that Jay trusted him was enough for me.

"Why did you lie to me before?" he asked me.

"You expected me to tell you the truth just because you asked me?"

"Look, sir, I have the responsibility of an entire country o my shoulders. Both countries are important to me. I couldn't t get out of either of these obligations. I can't abondon my people to work here, nor could I leave my duties here to I could lead my people. What would you have me do?"

"How am I supposed to believe you? You lied to me before. You could be lying now."

What he said was fair. Betrayal around here was taken very seriouslly. "Consider yourself in my position. What would you have done di-ferently?" I looked at him.

He opened his mouth several times to speak but remained quiet. "There was no other way. I did what I thought was best to keep my military obligation and protect my country, but now I need your help. So will you help me?"

"I suppose I will need to," Breeden said thoughtfully.

I was happy to hear this.

"You will help me?"

"Yes, but first, I need you to tell me everything from the start."

I knew exactly what he meant, so I started talking.

The Salvation

After I finished talking with Breeden, he sat there for a while quietly. He needed time so I sat with him. I didn't know what he was thinking but somehow I felt relieved. Even though I was the queen of Ashanti, I was still a citizen of the States. He was in power, and if there was a solution, he was the one who could find it.

"So, you became the queen because your father made a deal with the gods of your land that would spare the sacrifice of his son?" Breeden asked.

I could tell he was trying to calm himself. He was a good at person but he was very much opposed to these kinds of beliefs. He once told me he joined the navy because he wanted to do good in the world. If there was anyone in the navy who would help me, it was him. "Yes. I know how it sounds, but that's just the tradition of my land. We mut follow it."

"So, you gave the location of the operation site in Liberia?" he said, looking betrayed. "What else?"

"I did. Look, you know that the only people who died in those missions were innocent civilians. I wanted to save them." I wanted to be clear that this wasn't done because I had to betray America but to save lives.

"I see. Well it was a failed mission on your part. Even though I didn't want them to carry out that mission, I had no choice," he said more to himself than to me.

"Sir, we need to get Jelani out of whatever hole they are keeping him. It's the only thing I am worried about," I said, a hint of desperation in my voice. He was facing torture because of me. I needed to make that right.

"Look, I need to tell you one thing. This is out of my hands. I did not have him taken," he said.

Even he looked troubled by the thought of one of his men going through this. I needed to capitalize on that. "Sir, if there is anyone who can do this, it is you," I said. Even though I could have the general conduct a covert operation to rescue Jay, I knew that this would destroy his life and mine. Breeden was sympathetic, he would never stand for this.

"What would you have me do?" he asked.

"Sir, Jay is a good man. He's your man. I know that my situation is fucked up ," I said. I had never sworn in front of Breeden, but the situation had pushed me to desperation . "I need you to find a way. You owe him that much."

"I don't owe him anything. You did this," he said in anger. And I felt the guilt and shame instantly. He looked at me and was quiet for some time before answering. "If there is something to be done about this, it will have to be done on the admiral's orders," he said and didn't bother to elaborate.

He went on, "Oh, yes, I think we need to disclose your situation to the admiral. He and the rest of the chain are the only ones who can help nw and even if they can, the president will also get involved. This concerns national security. There is just no way around it."

Deep down, I had known this day would come but I didn't want to accept it. Now that everything was out in the open it scared me. This could go either way. It could either begin a never-ending war, or it could be my salvation. "How would you do that? How are you going to explain this to them." I asked him.

"We both know that the president will not be listening to any-one from this office, considering how our missions have been going."

"What the hell do you mean?" I said and realized I may have been a bit out of line.

He looked at me wih disapproval "Okay, I'm going to let that slide," he said. "But yes, we need to involve the chief of naval operations and we need to do it now."

"Hold on, what are you going to tell him?"

"I'm not telling him anything. You are going to tell him what you just told me. Also, before Maya and Adelaide get taken, we need them to come with us."

He said and walked out of the door. I followed him out and caught up with him as he spoke on the phone. "Where's Maya and Adelaide?"

I told him where they were, and he relayed the location on the phone. "They are gongto bring them to the White House. I think it would be best if they were present when we tal about this," he said.

"Okay." Even though I had been in the White House many times, today felt utterly nerve-racking.

*****

He went in and I called Maya. "Listen, people are coming over to your house. I need you to go with them. They are bringing you to me. I'm here with Breeden," I said. "Tell Femi to leave now! Things just got a lot more complicated than I thought."

"What did you tell him?" I could hear Adelaide's voice in the background.

"Everything."

"There's someone here," she interrupted.

"Go with them. They are bringing you here," I said and hung up the call. I was worried about Femi. If they discovered him here, it would only complicate things further. After about fifteen minutes later,

Breeden called me in and then I suddenly remember who I was I was the queen of Ashanti. That was something I seemed to have forgotten lately. I was going to handle this situation. I went into the office feeling confident and looked at the man sitting across from me. He seemed much more angrier now than whn I fistmet him. I wondered what Breeden had said to hm.

"Asha, please sit." With palms sweaing I sat next o Breeden "Please tell him what you told me,"

Through countless experiences, I had learned that nervousness was a part of the action. You would always feel nervous before going on a mission. However, when the mission started, it would all disap-pear. You moved your body like a machine, and that was the sensation that gripped me when I started talking. I told him everything that I had told Breeden. The CNO had the same reaction Breeden had and was silent for a long time before saying anything else. "Who else knows about this?" He had just asked this when someone entered the room.

"Sir, they're here," a man said, looking at us.

"Please send them in."

My friends walked in and I felt sick seeing pain across their faces. I told them Breeden knew of their involvement. Being asked now, I was unsure of what to say. I had no way of knowing what they might have said. I was afraid.

And before I could utter a word, "We all knew, sir. She said nothing but we knew, and we protected her." Adelaide answered.

I said shortly after her. "Sir, Jay needs to be released."

"Look, Asha, this is potentially war-starting situation but we can only try to fix it. Breeden has already told me what he thinks, and I agree. The president is going to get involved, but there is going to be a full investigation starting with you two," he said pointing to Maya and Adelaide. "Jay cannot be released until after we've talked with the President. He may agree to our solution for this madness. Now get out and stay away from the media. You're not to return home or draw any attention to yourselves until this is resolved. Understood?"

"Yes, sir!" the three of us responded instantly. "Leave us, Maya stay back for a few" he said to both Adelaide and me.

We were waiting outside for Maya, and after an hour she finally walked out. I had known her for a long time. It terrified and saddened me to have placed her in this position.. With this level of intensity regarding the situation, anything was possible. I looked at her, and just as I had thought, she looked to be angry. I walked toward her, but Breeden stopped me. He looked at Adelaide, and she walked in.

"Maya, are you okay?" I asked her. She nodded in response and sat down. I would have said something more, but she needed time. We waited for another two hours, and it was well after dark now. Adelaide came out looking exhausted and irritated.

"What did you tell him?" I asked.

"Everything" I felt my stomach tighten a bit more.

The CNO asked both Breeden and I to come into his office. When we entered, he was sitting in his chair and looked very trou-bled. "Asha, what you have done, who you are? This level of espio-nage and treason, amongst other crimes, has never been done since I started my career, and I am so inclined to bury you and your friends in the consequences of your actions." He paused. "However, I trust Breeden, and by extension I trust you too. I still need to tell the president about this. I cannot guarantee he will extend you the same understanding we're giving you. It already involves one head of a country, we need to involve the other. The matter of Jay will be solved in the meantime."

"So when are we going to meet with the president?" Breeden asked before I could open my mouth.

"Tomorrow. He's busy and cannot meet wih us at a moment's notice. Till then, I suggest that you all be taken somewhere safe and out of sight because I can't have this situation exposed. Should the public and other countries find out the chaos this news will cause, it will be immense. I cannot afford to have to explain that."

"Yes," Breeden replied and saluted him. We all followed suit and walked out of the room.

"So far, so good," Breeden said when we got to his office. "But that could all change after we meet with the president."

"What did you guys talk about when I was out of the room?" I asked him. Everything seemed to go a bit too smoothly, and it's made me nervous.

"When I was in the field, the CNO and I used to be close. We were on a covert mission together, which got a little complicated. He was up for a promotion and chose the mission above our safety. Thus, I was captured and totured when I made myself a target to ensure my team's survival. He feels he owes me for that. I'm the reason he's alive. I reminded him he has to settle a debt. I know you are an honorable person, Asha." He looked directly at me. "I trust you enough to believe you've told me the truth. I will go as far as possible to ensure Jay is safe and your situation is resolved."

I had no words. For the first time since this situation exploded, I was sure that I had trusted the right person. "Thank you, sir. I'm indebted."

"I know." He smiled.

If there was anyone I had no problem owing, it was him. I was about to reply when my phone rang. "Hey, Mom, I'm busy. Is it something important?" I asked.

"It is," she sounded worried.

"I was in a meeting with the elders, and Elder Kojo told everyone about your covert missions. He told everyone that your missions have been to oppose and destroy our sister countries and Ghana as a whole. Asha, what is going on? He has the details of the missions."

"What are you talking about? Mom, none of my covert mis-sions have been near or in Ghana. What is Kojo talking about?" I was already struggling to escape my current fate; the last thing I needed was this.

"He told the elders you conducted the killing of one of the tribal leaders in Brong-Ahafo. People died Asha an he's saying"

"Look, I have conducted no missions in Ghana. What did Elder Kofi say about this?"

"He reminded thm you were still their Queen Asha, you need to come home now."

"Mom, I'm not coming back right now. I have some matters here that I need to take care of. You need you to figue it out"

I called Femi and thankfully, he answered immediately.

"What is going on?" he sounded worried so i just went on with it and told hime what ou mum had told me.

"You need to go back home and handle the situation.

"Femi I cant, I need to see things through on this end."

"Promise me that as soon as things go awry, you'll call me. I will get you out before you can blink your eyes."

"Thanks, Femi, but I am optimistic about this."
"Alright," he said and hung up. I went back inside the room, and Breeden looked at me. "It's my mom, shemisses me." I said half truthfully.

"Maybe it would be best if we all rest our eyes for a bit," he sugested and we all nodded in agreement.

The threeof us went back to my house and thy both fell asleep as soon astey closed ther eyes but sleep would not come to me.

*****

162

Commander Breeden and I, along with the CNO reported to the White House. To my surprise, my mother, Elder Kofi, the general, and some of my political leaders were all present, waiting for me along with the president and some American diplomats. The room was filled with more titled men and women than I had ever dreamed of meeting. Never once did I think I would meet the entire military chain of command especially under these circumstances.

"We all know why we're here," the CNO began as the entire room turned and looked in my direction.

"How did this even happen?" the Secretary of State questioned. Then the president spoke. "Our focus here today is how our two countries can benefit from this situation and contain it without things getting out of hand."

My mother sucked her teeth in disgust and exclaimed, "To put it blatantly, she needs to come back and rule her kingdom."

"To put it blatantly, it's not that simple."

I could sense the disgust in his tone.

"Why not?"

"She has an obligation here with us. We can't just let her go," the CNO interjected.

My mom countered, "Well, I think we can all agree these are different circumstances, don't you think?"

"Maybe so, but had she been honest with us, maybe things wouldn't have gotten to this point."

"Well, we're here now," My mums tone began to worry me.

"That's on her, not us."

As they continued to exchange words, I became annoyed. "Everyone, shut up!" I yelled. The room fell silent immediately followed by stares from everyone. "I mean everyone needs to calm down," I said more calmly.

"Lieutenant, while we all respect your status back in your country, keep in mind everyone here outranks you greatly."

"Let's remember our military bearing. Is that understood?" the CNO said while he stared at me with disappointment. Elder Kofi interjected before I could even respond. "Our queen bows to no one."

"Uh, actually on this side of the water, yeah, she does."

"Nana, I cannot take this. This was a waste of time," Elder Kofi said as he stood up to leave.

"Elder, sit down!" I commanded him.

Breeden stood up and spoke on my behalf. "Lieutenant Osie is an impeccable leader and an outstanding sailor. In all my eighteen years of service, I've met no one as hardworking as her. It's true, our current dilemma seems unrecoverable. To do anything other than assisting her and her country in times like this will be nothing short of betrayal, as she has been nothing but an exceptional addition to our Navy."

"I've only met her once before this situation, and it was when she received her award. She truly must be a remarkable sailor to have received that award and ranked so high amongst her peers."

Once again the CNO spoke. My mother took a sip of water as tears fell from her eye. "There's a saying in the Twi language that when translated to English goes: 'A child who knows how to wash their hands eats with the elders.' My daughter has been eating with adults her entire life. Meaning, she has always been prepared for more extraordinary things, ever since her childhood. She has broken so many barriers that not even I thought was possible.

"She didn't have a say regarding this fate. We chose it for her, yet she has accepted it with grace and humility, and each day she reigns brings hope and restores faith to our people. We need her. Inct i think we bth do. The words my mother spoke touched us all.

My entire life, I'd sought to be better and strive for greatness. My life path had already been created for me even before I was born and I was paying for it. Destiny had allowed me to be something unique but now everyone needed me. Selfishly, a part of me wanted the navy to deny the request my people were making. The navy had been my life since I was old enough to be considered an adult. Leaving the service would affect me I was I couldnt fathom. Was I selfish for wanting to be a part of both parallel worlds? A voice brought me back to reality.

"I've heard you all. While Lieutenant Osie's contract in the mil-itary is not over, we cannot ignore the facts of the circumstances." The discovery of her identity by the wrong people could prove dangerous to us, not to mention the questions that would arise if her shipmates were to find out. We also cannot ignore her royal status, as it would bring distrust from her people.

"Because of this complicated situation, her remaining two years active-duty will be amended. I will send her on a temporary duty assignment in Djibouti as our liaison in foreign affairs. From there, she will be required to physically check in once a month, start-ing next month, until her two years are over.

"In the meantime, she may return to her country and rule as their queen immediately. A press statement will be released here only to people on a need-to-know basis. Should you make a press release, nothing regarding your contract's amendment or details regarding our missions may be included. Such an action would render this agreement obsolete. You may address your subjects regarding your military life and nothing more. Once your two years is over, an official statement will be made to the public detailing everything. In return for our support, we will require intel should there be an attack from any of the other countries in Africa against the US."

"With all due respect, sir, I cannot be your spy," I objected immediately.

"I believe the right word is an ally. We support you on any mat-ters you have, and you do the same, at least till the two years are up. This will ensure the existence of a mutually beneficial relationship. Those are our terms," he concluded.

"We accept," my mother said as she nudged me.
"Very well then. It was a pleasure to meet you all. Lieutenant, take care. I trust that you will let the commander know should you need anything," the president said, looking over at Breeden as he walked out.

"Yes, sir." I shook my head in agreement, smiled at Breeden, and walked out with my people.

*****

We headed home in victory as I prepared myself for exactly what I would tell my people regarding their concerns about wht had happened.

The Unborn

I finished speaking and waited for a bit. The entire room was dead silent, and then suddenly, the whole audience broke out in applause, which was joined by my elders and family. The foreigners didn't understand the complexities of our nation and were oblivious to the needs of carrying out the traditions we practiced. I told them everything. Why and how I became queen instead of my brother. why I had been visiting the United States, and how I had established a lifelong relationship with the United States.

This was a huge thing, having the United States support you. and I was overly optimistic that our country would now make strides toward brightening the future like never before. I stepped aside when the applause didn't stop. I looked back and saw Femi trying his best to hide his smile.

They were still applauding, and I got off the podium and waved to them. I promptly ignored the crowd as they rushed toward me and walked back to sit down so that Femi could speak.

He got on the podium, and after the applause died down, he said, "That was very touching, Your Majesty. Since you have pretty much addressed everything, there will be no questions." He walked toward the elders and then said, "Let us all head to the palace for dinner."

*****

On the way to dinner, I wondered what kind of reaction me telling them about everything would get, but I was now put to ease. They were all cheering, and I couldn't have been happier.

However, there was still dinner to get through before the dip-lomats and my friends would go back. I looked around and saw that Jay remained in the back, out of my reach. I wanted to talk to him personally. We all took our seats starting with me. I kept stealing glances toward Jay, hoping that he would catch my eyes once, but he seemed determined to ignore me. I knew this was a just punishment for the last time we talked. *How was I supposed to let him know how much I loved him when there was nothing I could do? How was I supposed to tell him he was the person I wanted to spend the rest of my life with?* These thoughts were depressing me, and I was losing composure. On the one hand, my country and sovereign reign were utterly secure, yet I couldn't choose the person I wanted to marry.

After dinner was over, the diplomats were escorted back to their cars for return. Jay, Maya, Adelaide, and Breeden were all pretending that I didn't exist, which hurt me significantly. I couldn't understand why they were acting this way. Everything was beautiful now. I didn't have to hide my true identity from anyone. My friends should at least hang back for two days so they could cel-ebrate my victory with me. At the very least they could pretend to be happy for me. I went back to my room, still confused about what the issue was. When I opened the door, my mother and Elder Kofi waited for me, along with Femi, who was grinning uncontrollably.

*****

"Elder Kofi, thank you," I said and went forward to hug him. I knew that tradition didn't call for a queen to hug an elder, but I supposed I was done with traditions for today. Elder Kofi was the reason I was le negotiate a better contract with the navy.

"I live to serve you, my queen," he replied, letting go of me.

I looked at my mother and hugged her too.

"You are the best ruler this country has ever seen. Maybe even better than your father."

I stepped back and looked at her wide-eyed.

"Oh, yes! He would have been proud to see what his daughter is accomplishing now. I want you to know that I am with you no matter what happens, and I will support you. Today, you have proven that you are truly your father's daughter. Only he could think of something so mad, and only you could carry it out so gracefully. I am proud of you, Asha," This was one of those rare moments when she talked to me as both her daughter and leader.

"Thank you, Mum, I couldn't have done any of it without you. Oh, and Femi, we need to take care of our dear uncle. None of this would have ever happened if not for him."

"Yes, don't worry about that. I didn't forget about it," he said, the smile melting off his face for a second before it returned.

"We would like to tell you something, my queen." He nudged Elder Kofi.

"I haven't forgotten. I was just getting to it," Kofi said, smiling warmly toward me.

I looked at him, and I tried to guess what was going on.

"We have realized that we were quick to judge your friends," Elder Kofi began. "They have proven valuable and very loyal. Femi told us that neither of them betrayed you while they were being investigated regarding your identity. Jay is an honorable man and someone who has become very dear to the people of Kumasi—"

"Mostly because his Twi is so funny. People need a laugh around here," Femi interrupted, and my mother laughed, lightly slapping him.

I couldn't believe my ears. *Were they going to let me marry him?* I was so surprised, and even though I kept calm, they knew that I was

169

at a loss for words. Femi walked forward and held me by my shoulders and turned me around.

There, standing at the door, was Jelani, along with my two best friends. He was smiling at me, that adorable smile that always lit up when he looked at me. I had to refrain when I saw him earlier at dinner, but not anymore. I ran forward before anyone coud stop me. I hugged him fiercely, and he groaned. I didn't have any words, and it seemed like he didn't either.

"They have set the wedding for the month after next so that everyone can take part," my mother said, putting a hand over my shoulder and nodding at Adelaide.

"Now, my queen, if you will excuse us," Femi said and led everyone out of the room, leaving Jay and me alone. That entire night was spent confessing just how much we missed each other and how happy we were that we could finally be together.

*****

The day of the wedding arrived in the blink of an eye. It felt like it was just yesterday I had conducted a meeting with the American diplomats, and now I was getting married. I had just woken up, though I'd barely slept at all. I was way too excited, and it was almost time for me to get up and shower. I had been swamped the past few days, getting every traditional skin treatment and ritual so I could "remain the most beautiful queen and live a long and happy life," or so they said. I rushed into the bathroom and took a bath.

This was going to be a traditional wedding, and Jay had agreed to do everything the Ghanaian way. He was happy to oblige our traditions and customs. I went to speak with Femi and my mother. "I need a favor from you." I said. I knew they were too busy with their preparations. Femi was in charge of my security and safety while my mother took care of everything else. "No," both of them said in unison and laughed.

"Great. So you guys need to educate Jay about Ghanaian traditions. We need to satisfy the elders and the people—most importantly, the high priest. We need to prove that even though I am mar-rying an American by culture, he's an African by blood," I said.

"Well, tht's most important," my mother said. They both looked serious and nodded to each other.

"Don't worry. He's a fast learner," Femi joked. Recently, Jay had become inseparable from my mother and Femi. We didn't get to see each other for some days because of the preparations. His entire family were come to Kumasi, and I had already arranged for their stay in the palace.

I had met Jay's father in the past, but our relationship never allowed us to be formally introduced to each other's parents. I was nervous for reasons I couldn't understand. When I Finally met them, both familes joined together for dinner. His father laughed and joked about his son's childhood mischief and congratulated us on our union.

*****

The preparation for the wedding had pushed everyone to their very limits of organizational skill. If it weren't for my mother and brother, my wedding would never have been possible, along with the general. Heads of states from almost fifty countries were going to attend the royal wedding, including the president of the United States, the president of Russia, the queen of England, the royal family of Saudi Arabia, and Royalty from all over the world. All of them were here to be part of my history.

They had decorated the entire palace in white and gold, and the wedding was to take place in the garden in front of the palace. My royal wedding dress was a traditional dress made of kente fabric that Ghanaians wore. The loom of the fabric is made in such a way that different-colored threads are laced through it. It can be woven into layers and patterns. My dress was simple but intricate. I had it specially made to honor my culture.

After so many hurdles, here I was, a success. The dress was woven in different colors, as was the custom in Ashanti: blue, which meant harmony, balance, and space; green, meaning growth and rebirth; gold, meaning financial, spiritual, or intellectual wealth and royalty; gray, meaning healing and cleansing; black, meaning spiritual elevation and maturation; white representing new beginnings; red and brown, representing earth; and silver standing for serenity. All these intricate threads were woven carefully together. It made the dress even more exquisite.

After donning the dress and having my makeup and hair done, I could hardly believe it was me. I had gotten so used to being in military clothes, I'd forgotten what it felt like to wear anything else.

Another tradition that the Ghanaians people followed was called *kokako*, which was the knocking ceremony. This was the first step in initiating a marriage process and symbolized respect for and unification of two families. When the maids informed Jay's family, we were ready. The elders, the high priest, my family, and anyone who mattered sat down waiting for the official *kokooko*. I looked at them, and they stared at me wide-eyed.

My mother was the first to recover. "Asha, come here, quick!" she ordered me. After waiting for a while, Jay's family knocked on the door; an elder ushered for them to enter, and they formally asked for my hand in marriage. Jay had arranged for several gifts to be delivered to my family. Along with that came my bride's price and traditional items requested by the elders. My brother and Elder Kofi stepped in as a father figure alongside my mother. The gifts comprised of things like goats, clothes, jewelry, a mat, a stool, cola nuts, and palm wine, and many more. They accepted the items on my behalf. Soon after, everyone in the room cheered, and the maids brought in liba-tions to consecrate the union.

I was blown away by how handsome Jay looked in traditional royal clothes. I had requested our clothes be made from the same fabrics. We celebrated and then left the room for the official royal wedding in the garden.

After that, the traditional ceremony began. It was filled with laughter, dance, and food. While they followed our customs to appease my people, my mother had decided that this was to be held at daybreak so that our lives would be filled with light and happiness. We led the way to the aisle, walking among some of the most influ-ential people in the world. A sense of fear engulfed me as I remembered the secret I had been holding on to amidst all the chaos. Femi had taken notice of my feverish look and weight loss because of my severe morning sickness; I wondered what my people would say if they were to find out I was pregnant before my marriage. How would Jay react? My friends? and most of all my mother! How could I ever explain this to my elders? They would forbid this union and reject my unborn child. They would never forgive me for this. As fear raced through my body, my father's words encouraged me: "Queens don't cry. They prevail," As the words danced in my mind, I felt a sense of hope.

About the Author

Nana Aba, traditionally known as Antaba is a Ghanaian Poet, Writer and the author of the well-anticipated YA Fictional book "Stolen Heritage" which publishes November 16th 2021.

As a Ghanaian native raised in the heart of Central Region, Ghana. Her family migrated to the United States and settled in Erie, Pennsylvania under the refugee program. As the first female born among three siblings, She is heavily relied upon to support her family. At a young age, she began writing as an escape. With the burden of adapting to an entirely new culture and dealing with an immigrant's struggles, she was determined to excel and made an impressive impact on her peers and everyone she encountered.

She is also the creator of the "Quality Chat" Blog, offering inspiration, hope, mentorship, and motivational coaching to young people all over the world. As the first and only female author in her tribe, she uses her writing to capture the beauty and power of her culture by creating stories that not only teach others of the African heritage but promote resiliency, courage, and empowerment.